Cycling in Clydesdale

Paul Lamarra

Published by Sigma Leisure – an imprint of
Sigma Press, 1 South Oak Lane, Wilmslow, Cheshire SK9 6AR, England.

British Library Cataloguing in Publication Data
A CIP record for this book is available from the British Library.

ISBN: 1-85058-779-5

Typesetting and Design by: Sigma Press, Wilmslow, Cheshire.

Cover Design: Linda Dawes

Photographs: Main cover picture – in the shadow of Tinto; small pictures (from top to bottom) – At the crossroads, Carmichael; Scottish flag; On the road to Auchengray. *(All photographs by Paul Lamarra)*

Maps: Jeremy Semmens

Printed by: MFP Design and Print

Disclaimer: the information in this book is given in good faith and is believed to be correct at the time of publication. No responsibility is accepted by either the author or publisher for errors or omissions, or for any loss or injury howsoever caused. Only you can judge your own fitness, competence and experience.

Preface

Ten years ago, I began cycling with friends as a way of keeping fit in between climbing trips. Every other weekend we would make forays into Clydesdale. Slowly, I became acquainted with the numerous back roads that criss-cross this beautiful and tranquil landscape. From the dyke-lined lanes through classic farmland scenes to high un-fenced hill roads, Clydesdale has much to offer the cyclist and is so easily reached by a large proportion of the Scottish populace.

The old churches, ruined towers, monuments and castles that say so much about what went on here, and are off the well-beaten tourist trails, intrigued me. Clydesdale played an important part in Scottish history from the Bronze Age, through Wallace to the industrial revolution. I hope that this guide helps to fill in the gaps for the exploring and interested cyclist.

It was only when cycling abroad in areas feted for their idyllic cycling that I realised Clydesdale was woefully under exploited by cyclists. Many people asked, "Where is it you go on your bike?" Many were dubious as to whether there was pleasurable cycling to be enjoyed so close to industrialised central Scotland. Therefore, it was with this in mind that I decided to write this book.

My aim has been to provide a guide that provides the necessary information for cyclists to make the right choice of trip – whether it is a family looking for a safe and entertaining day out or the seasoned cyclist looking for a challenge or a new area to explore.

I never cease to enjoy a day out on the bike in Clydesdale and am regularly accompanied by my young family. I hope that this guide will entice those many people who own a bike but don't know where to use it.

I would like to thank the following for their generous assistance: Janice Govan, Rev. Bev Gauld, Cllr. Eddie McAvoy, Simon Pilpel and South Lanarkshire Council, Cllr. Addison, Scottish Natural Heritage, Grace Nichol at SUSTRANS, Scottish Power, Scottish Wildlife Trust, Dr. Ian Hamilton Finlay, Hugh Murray, Stewart Love, Vincent Lunny, Richard Carmichael of Carmichael, Gerard McCosh, ScotRail, Claire Loughran, John and May Lamarra. Special thanks to my wife Catherine and her late father Harry Kennedy.

Contents

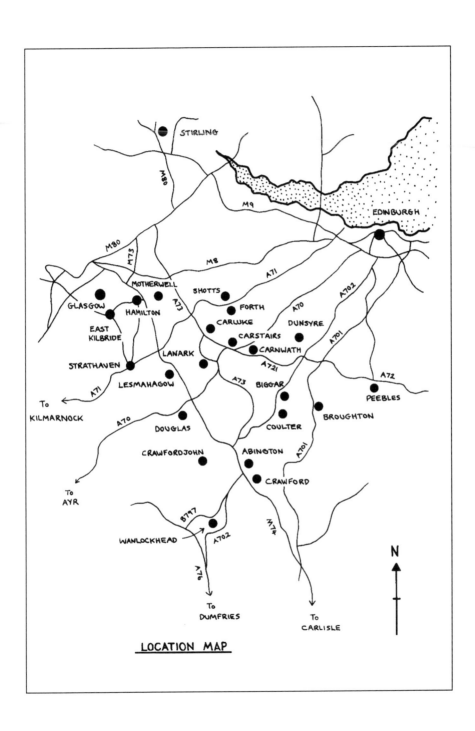

LOCATION MAP

Introduction

Using the Guide

In this book, 18 of the 21 routes are circular. Only the reservoir routes are linear and require you to retrace the outward route. I have described the routes in the direction that I have found through experience derives the greatest benefit from the prevailing wind and the terrain.

The circular routes are based on four base towns and villages, and there is a separate section for each set of routes. Each route has a preamble that gives a brief description, the distance, a guide to the terrain and possible links, all of which should allow you to decide on its suitability. For each town, there is some historical background and a visitor guide that highlights how to get there, where to eat and where to stay.

"By the Way" is a commentary on each route. It provides information on things to look out for, historical contexts and refreshment stops so that you get the most from each route. This is followed by detailed directions with a distance indicator and a simple map. Should you prefer to use the Ordnance Survey map, the grid reference of the point to which each set of instructions applies is also given in the detailed directions. When the progress between points is less than a quarter of a mile, the distance is omitted. When there is a definite destination to a route, such as Douglas, the directions are divided so that you can start at either location. The maps show each junction that you will encounter but only show the roads to be followed. Ideally, read "By the Way" at your leisure and take a copy of the detailed directions with you, suitably protected from the elements.

A Brief History of Clydesdale

I have chosen the name Clydesdale to describe the southerly part of Lanarkshire, although some of the routes poke out of the edges into Ayrshire, Dumfries and Galloway and Scottish Borders. Clydesdale is an area of stunning natural beauty criss-crossed by meandering back roads that are ideal for peaceful cycling. It is in stark contrast to industrial Lanarkshire further to the north, to which Clydesdale is politically welded by the Clyde watershed marking the boundary. Within

Clydesdale there are contrasting landscapes. The Southern Upland Boundary Fault, which runs across Clydesdale from Crawfordjohn to Biggar, separates the gentle lowlands cut by the Clyde and its tributaries from the high rolling hills of the Southern Uplands with their wide glaciated valleys. Tinto Hill (2320 feet) is an igneous extrusion that stands alone to the north of the fault, a graceful peak that is synonymous with Clydesdale. Climbing Tinto Hill is a very popular day out.

Clydesdale has been a choice place to live for thousands of years, fertile land by the Clyde and small isolated hillocks that were ideal for necessarily defensive settlement, no doubt an irresistible combination to early migrants. Human occupation began about 8,000 years ago with the arrival of the Mesolithic (early Stone Age) people, evidence of whom has been found in the form of stone tools on the banks of the Clyde near Crawford. Later Neolithic settlers left a more definitive stamp, building settlements and starting the process of clearing woodland that leaves the largely treeless landscape we see today. Only inaccessible pockets of this ancient woodland remain notably in the Mouse and Craignethan Valleys.

Some of the most conspicuous evidence of early human presence on the landscape dates from the Bronze Age, the most striking example is the huge cairn that surmounts Tinto Hill. The Iron Age people were the most prodigious fort and settlement builders exploiting the hilltops and the discrete valleys. The remains of their distinctive circular forts with double ramparts are to be found all over Clydesdale. One of the easiest to detect is on the lower slopes of Tinto at Fallburn. The Iron Age ceased with the arrival of the Romans. The Romans came in three waves, once under the orders of Flavian in AD110 and twice under Antonine between AD139 and AD161. The Romans attempted and failed to quell the northern tribes on each of these occasions but they built many forts and camps and the roads to link them in the process. The biggest fort was at Castledykes, to the East of Lanark near Ravenstruther.

Constantine legalised Christianity and, although the Romans had departed, southern Scotland still fell under this influence. St Ninian famously converted the southern Picts. St Ninian's well and chapel at Lamington and the ancient chapel at Warrenhill, Covington, hint at the presence of his fifth-century mission in Clydesdale. St Kentigern followed up St Ninian's good work and he may have been based in Broughton for a time, and possibly baptising local resident Merlin.

David I patronised the anglicised Normans and Flemings, giving them land in return for their support; he also introduced the feudal system of government. The Lords were given the right to raise taxes from tenants – who in turn would expect protection – appoint a priest and try criminals. Culter Motte Hill is a good example of the Norman brand of settlement and can be visited on 'The Round of Biggar Common'.

As trade developed with the rest of Europe in the 12th century, the King granted charters to create Royal Burghs. The charter allowed the town to hold weekly markets and a number of fairs each year. Lanark is one of the oldest of the 66 Royal Burghs, receiving its charter in 1140. Royal Burghs could not deal with the burgeoning trade, so the privileges were widened to Burghs of Barony. Charters were granted to local barons to hold markets, but foreign goods had to be purchased from a Royal Burgh. Many Burghs of Barony were created in Clydesdale, Biggar and Carnwath in the 15th century and Carluke and Lesmahagow in the 17th century. Burghs of Barony such as Crawfordjohn and Roberton failed to attract much trade and remained tiny hamlets.

Rich in resources, the 18th and 19th centuries saw Clydesdale playing a prominent part in the Industrial Revolution. Mining for lead and coal was stepped up, the Clyde was harnessed to power the mills built by David Dale and Richard Arkwright, the Wilson brothers opened their cutting-edge iron works and the shale oil industry thrived at Tarbrax. All of these activities had a major impact on the surrounding landscapes. New communities with new values were created in places where people were unaccustomed to living, spoil heaps of all shades dotted the countryside and railways reached into almost every corner. Despite being feted for the forward and altruistic thinking that accompanied industrial development in Clydesdale, industry died a slow death. Today, industrial heritage and tourism along with agriculture are Clydesdale's mainstays.

The Killing Times, 1662-1688

A feature of the Clydesdale landscape is the number of memorials to Covenanters who were executed for their beliefs. They fought to be free of patronage and government interference in their religion and set out to establish Presbyterianism throughout Britain and Ireland.

The high lonely moors were popular spots for the gathering of Covenanters to worship God and to hear their "outed" Ministers preach. These gatherings were known as conventicles. They were sought out

and ruthlessly put down by
the government. The need to
hold conventicles arose from
Charles II's wish to impose
bishops and patronage on the
Presbyterian Church of Scotland in 1662.

> *The Solemn League and Covenant*
> *Cost Scotland Blood, cost Scotland tears*
> *But it sealed freedom's sacred cause*
> *If thou'rt a slave, indulge thy sneers*
>
> **– Robert Burns**

In 1638 many ministers of the Church of Scotland and noblemen
had signed the "National Covenant" and in 1643 the "Solemn League
and Covenant" with the English Parliamentarians, hence Covenanters.
The Covenant of 1638 was in response to Charles I and Bishop Laud's
desire to impose a new prayer book, "Laud's Liturgy" and episcopacy on
the Presbyterian Church. Through signing the Covenant, the signato-
ries pledged themselves to maintain the true religion free of patronage.
These events precipitated the Bishops' Wars of 1639-1641.

In 1662, those who supported the Covenant did not take too kindly
to yet another attempt by a Stuart King to control the Church of Scotland. Therefore, 270 of the ministers who were obliged to resign and
apply to Charles II's bishops to be reappointed, refused and undertook
open-air worship in defiance. These were the "outed" ministers. A 1665
Act banned conventicles under pain of fine, imprisonment or corporal
punishment. The Pentland Rising followed in 1666 but the
Covenanters were defeated at Rullion Green.

Two attempts at reconciliation attracted some ministers back to
their parishes but those who still refused suffered even harsher repres-
sion, which only strengthened their cause. By 1678 south-west Scotland was particularly out of government control and so "The Highland
Host", 6000 Highland and 3000 Lowland troops were sent in to maintain order. The heavy-handed approach made revolt even more likely
and, in June 1679, an armed conventicle defeated government troops
under James Graham of Claverhouse at Drumclog. Buoyed by this
victory 4000 Covenanters gathered on the banks of the Clyde at Hamilton three weeks after Drumclog. Success was short lived. The
Covenanters who gathered were heavily defeated by the forces of the
Duke of Monmouth in the Battle of Bothwell Bridge.

The Duke of Monmouth initiated a third attempt at reconciliation
but some still refused to submit and organised themselves into a group
known as the Cameronians under the command of hard-line
Covenanters Richard Cameron and Donald Cargill.

Cameron and Cargill were behind the "Declaration of Sanquhar" of 1680, denouncing their allegiance to the King. One month after the declaration the Cameronians were defeated at Aird's Moss in Ayrshire and Cameron was killed. Cargill was captured near Covington (Route 1) and hanged in Edinburgh in 1681. James VII, who came to the throne in 1685, allowed Presbyterians to worship in their own way but he did not extend an amnesty to the Cameronians. James Renwick, a Cameronian Minister was the last to be executed in 1688.

1690 saw William and Mary of Orange on the throne and parliamentary approval of the Presbyterian form of church government, but the National Covenant was disregarded. The Cameronians continued to support the Covenant and, in 1712, their Minister John McMillan renewed the Covenants on Auchensaugh Moor (between Douglas and Crawfordjohn). Despite also excommunicating Queen Anne and her parliament, the events went largely unnoticed.

What's in a Name?

In Clydesdale, just as in every other locality, the pronunciation of some place names defies all the rules. If you mispronounce, locals will either put you right with glee, as they are very proud of these peculiarities, or pretend not to know to where you are referring. Kilncadzow is pronounced *kilcaigie*, Strathaven is pronounced *straiven* and Ravenstruther is pronounced *rinstrie*. The major *faux pas* relates to the River Mouse – it is known as *The Moose* in these parts. As far as I know, everywhere else is pronounced the way you would expect.

The suffix *-ton* is very common in the southerly part of Clydesdale. The *tons* were the lands belonging to the new Fleming Lords. Thankerton, Lamington, Wiston, Covington were the lands of Tancard, Lambin, Wice and Colban, respectively.

A common prefix in the northerly part of Clydesdale is *Car-*, e.g. Carnwath, Carstairs and Carluke. This is thought to be derived from the Cumbric word *cair* meaning fort or the Gaelic *carn* meaning a cairn.

Cycling

Preparation

It is all too easy just to jump on the bike and go. I often fall into this trap and live to regret it. An enjoyable day out is more likely if your bike is properly maintained. Check your bike over before you cycle. Tighten

Unveiling a National Cycle Network milepost alongside the B7078 near Lesmahagow

anything that's loose that shouldn't be, check the brakes and see that the chain is clean and well lubricated. Properly inflated tyres are essential for efficient cycling.

None of the routes in this book is off-road, so if you own a mountain bike with knobbly tyres but never really cycle off-road you may want to consider smooth road tyres. You will notice an enormous difference if you have been persevering with the knobbly ones. Using the gears effectively will also extend the length of route that you can manage.

What to Wear? What to Carry?

Specialised cycling clothing is not necessary but you will do well to choose clothes that mimic their qualities. Shorts or trousers that are quick drying and that permit easy movement are best – but they shouldn't be so loose that there is a danger of them becoming entangled. Gloves are a good idea even on a good day, fingerless gloves are inexpensive, as they protect your hands in a fall and they delay the onset of pressure points. Shoes with a stiff sole will offer the most comfort.

Let the weather be your guide. In cold weather, wear lots of thin layers that can be peeled away as you warm up. In summer, wear clothes that let air circulate freely. Clydesdale's weather is a lot drier than people think, but it's best to carry a light waterproof, as it is sure to rain if you leave it behind. Opinion is divided on whether wearing a helmet should be compulsory but I would err on the side of caution and wear one anyway.

It is essential that you carry a puncture repair kit, tyre levers and a pump but it is also a good idea to carry one or two spare inner tubes. A lightweight multi-purpose spanner should also be included and the relevant Allen keys. Bitter experience has persuaded me to carry spare chain links and a link extractor. A bicycle lock is always a good idea.

Most importantly, carry something to eat that will replace lost energy and plenty of water – on hot days, take special care to avoid dehydrating, as it's easily done.

Safety

Following this basic advice will contribute to a safe day's cycling:

- Acquaint yourself with the Highway Code.
- Cycle two-abreast but in single file when visibility is restricted, when fording a stream or crossing narrow bridges.
- Restrain your momentum when descending if the visibility is restricted or there is the possibility of livestock on the road. Livestock is frequently on the move between enclosed fields, so be patient.
- Wear bright, highly visible clothing and wear a helmet.
- If it is at all possible that you will have to cycle after dark ensure that you have lights in working order fitted to your bike.
- Do not overload your bike and try to use luggage specifically manufactured for cycling. If you are using panniers take care to ensure that the load is balanced and put the heaviest items to the bottom.
- Be aware of other road users, many of the back roads are also used by pedestrians and people on horseback. Do not cycle on pavements!
- Warn each other of impending hazards – e.g. shout, 'hole' and point to it.

Cycling with Children

I have cycled many of the routes with my own children on-tow in a trailer or in a child seat. Older children will be able to tackle some of the routes under their own steam. I suggest you avoid Routes 3, 5, 6, 11, 13, 14 and 18 with children. Also, I avoid the section of the A70 between Carstairs Village and Ravenstruther on Route 1. Extra special care is required when cycling with children and it is a good idea to take measures to make them more visible – like attaching a flag to their bike or trailer and always cycling just slightly behind them so you can keep an eye on them.

My children love a day out on the bikes but I have learned many hard lessons while cycling with them. Try not to attempt more than an hour's cycling at a time, have another purpose to the day that will motivate them (e.g. a picnic or a visit to a park), keep a check on their comfort and remember children can tire very quickly – so have a fall-back plan.

Carmichael Estates

Carmichael Estates provide a range of facilities for visitors. Cyclists are welcome at their self-catering cottages and at the Carmichael Visitor Centre on the A73 south of the Hyndford Bridge, you can also make a detour to it from Route 1. There is a farm shop, an exhibition telling Carmichael's story and a local produce tea-room/restaurant. The Estates are happy for patrons of their facilities to cycle on the private roads. Groups should contact the visitor centre in advance on (01899) 308169 or www.carmichael.co.uk.

Cycle Hire

There is, at present, no-one offering cycle-hire in Clydesdale but South Lanarkshire Council have plans to offer the facility at Biggar Public Park. Enquire on (01899) 223019 to get the up-to-date position.

Dales Cycles in Glasgow have a limited number of hybrids and mountain bikes for hire that come with all the necessary extras, for details contact them on 0141 332 2705.

Bike Trax in Edinburgh hire everything you could possibly need, including kiddie trailers, luggage and car racks, contact them on 0131 228 6333.

A Peebles company, Scottish Border Trails, organises cycle holidays but they also hire out bikes to individuals, SBT can be contacted on (01727) 722934.

Cycle Spares and Repairs

There is only one shop in Clydesdale that considers itself a cycle shop, some outdoor equipment and car part shops may sell a limited range of cycle spares.

Wm. Withers, 186 Hyndford Road, Lanark (opposite Lanark Loch); tel: (01555) 665878

The Lanark Routes

Lanark

Lanark is an intimate little market town that sits high above the Clyde on a classic defensive site, and it can trace its history back to Roman Times. Elevated to a Royal Burgh in 1140 by David I, Lanark entered its hey day. Lanark was en route for Kings wanting to visit the south west of their kingdom or the Upper Tweed Valley. William I and Alexander II were frequent visitors and Robert the Bruce was the patron of a Franciscan Friary that stood on the site where the Clydesdale Inn stands today. It was in 1183 that Pope Lucius III made reference to Lanark Grammar in a "Papal Bull", making it one of the oldest schools in Britain.

The Wellgate, Lanark

The claim to fame that Lanark prefers is that William Wallace is reputed to have wooed his wife Marion Braidfute in Lanark, having met her at the towns St Kentigern's Church. The ruin of St Kentigern's and its churchyard can be found at the end of Ladyacre Road opposite the Livestock Auction Market.

After a street skirmish involving Wallace and some English soldiers, garrisoned in Lanark, Edward I's sheriff, Heselrig, executed Marion, instead of her husband Wallace who had fled the scene. Wallace avenged her death by killing Heselrig and thus set himself on the path to rebellion against English occupation and becoming the hero of the Wars of Independence.

A statue of the stocky Wallace is incorporated into the clock tower of St Nicholas' Church at the foot of the High Street, a plaque opposite marks the spot of his home and a pub in the town is called the Wallace Cave. The actual cave believed to be Wallace's refuge after the skirmish is below the Cartland Bridge to the north of the town.

The medieval settlement pattern of burghage plots, long narrow strips of land fronted by a house onto the High Street, is still in evidence and can be appreciated by walking up one of the many medieval closes that lead off High Street. The medieval town was centred on an area known as the Castlegate and the Bloomgate. The oldest buildings are marked-out by their crow-stepped gables, a distinctively Scottish characteristic. The building that protrudes from the line of buildings at the foot of the High Street is the 18th-century tollbooth, which was the location of the town courtroom and gaol.

A book detailing three heritage walks is available at the Tourist Information Offices, just along from the rail and bus station. It points out all the buildings and features of note in the medieval town and on the impressive Victorian, Hope Street.

Lanark has a more diminished role today. It is no longer the seat of local government, its garrison is long abandoned as is the racecourse and it struggles to compete with its precocious offspring New Lanark for visitors.

New Lanark

New Lanark sits right by the Clyde as this was the source of power for the mills. New Lanark is about 250 feet lower than Lanark and is very quickly and effortlessly reached by bike. Leave Lanark railway station, turn left and then right at the Auction Market onto Hyndford Road then take second left onto Braxfield Road, which hooks back. Follow Braxfield Road downhill into New Lanark. The thought of the way back up may temper your enjoyment of the free-wheel.

A contender for the UNESCO World Heritage Site designation, it is a perfectly preserved 18th-century factory village in a stunning woodland setting by the River Clyde. The best view of the village is from the view-ing platform on the Clyde Walkway from Castlebank Park.

New Lanark began as a project initiated by Richard Arkwright and David Dale. Arkwright believed that New Lanark would become the Manchester of Scotland and by 1799 four mills were operational, employing 2000 people who were housed in the specially built tene-ment rows.

David Dale and his son-in-law Robert Owen brought the village to particular prominence with their programme of social improvement. For adults the Institute for the Formation of Character was set up, there was a school, a nursery, and a co-operative store, which was to serve as the prototype for the co-operative movement.

New Lanark went into decline after the mills closed in 1968 but thanks to an enthusiastic housing association and the New Lanark Conservation Trust, it is a thriving community and visitor attraction. Most of the tenements are now occupied, a large part of one row has been converted to an excellent youth hostel, there are the "see it as it was attractions", and one of the mills is now a first-class hotel. The Scottish Wildlife Trust has a base and Visitor Centre from which they manage the Falls of Clyde Nature Reserve. In addition, there are a number of speciality shops and a cafeteria.

Many footpaths start from New Lanark. The most popular walk is to the impressive Falls of Clyde, the Corra Linn (1 mile) and the Bonnington Linn (2 miles). It is possible to visit Bonnington Linn from the opposite bank with a detour from Routes 1 and 2.

Practical Information

Getting There

Lanark is the most easily accessed town in Clydesdale, within half-an-hour of the Central Belt and it has a railway link with Glasgow. New Lanark can only be accessed through Lanark.

Road

From Glasgow: follow the M74 to junction 7 Larkhall and follow the A72, "Clyde Valley Tourist Route", for 12 miles to Lanark. From the south: follow the M74 to junction 12 and follow the A70 over the Hyndford Bridge into Lanark. From Edinburgh: follow the M8 to junc-tion 6 Newhouse signed "Lanark & Airdrie" and follow A73 for 15 miles to Lanark via Newmains and Carluke. Alternatively follow the A70 west signed, "Ayr and Kilmarnock", through Juniper Green and Balerno to Carnwath ("The Lang Whang") and on through Carstairs to take up the A743 at Ravenstruther into Lanark.

Rail

There is one train an hour in and out of Lanark to Glasgow via Motherwell on the Argyll Line. Times of arrival and departure differ on a Sunday and you should check the timetable carefully. There is no specific space for bikes but Strathclyde Transport are happy for you to store them in the door area, but avoid peak times as the commuters are liable to lynch you.

Eating and Drinking

Lanark is most likely to offer the visitor a cup of tea, as there are at least half-a-dozen tea-rooms and cafés. Those with a no-smoking policy or a separate area for smokers, are in the minority. Castlebank Park (turn left at St Nicholas' Church) with its impressive oaks and chestnut trees is a good choice for a picnic as is the park at Lanark Loch (follow A73 out of Lanark, signed Carlisle, for ½ mile). There is also a large family friendly restaurant/pub adjacent to Lanark Loch and a snack bar, which opens during the summer months.

There are public houses that offer good ales and bar meals, notably the Horse and Jockey on High Street, the Wallace Cave on the Broomgate, the Clydesdale Inn (a former coaching inn) and the Crown Hotel on Hope Street opposite the Sheriff Court. The Auction Market Restaurant when open will provide hearty meals to farmers and cyclists alike.

Staying

Accommodation is a bit sparse in Lanark with only five B&Bs in the town and one hotel. In New Lanark, however there is an excellent SYHA youth hostel (Contact (01555) 666710) and the upmarket New Lanark Hotel. Campsites are to be found in Kirkfieldbank about one mile from the station (downhill) and on the A70 at Newhouse between Ravenstruther and Carstairs Village. Full details can be obtained by contacting the all year round Tourist Information Centre in Lanark on (01555) 661661 or lanark@seeglasgow.com.

1. On Tintock-tap there is a mist

There may well be mist on Tinto as the first line of a mysterious poem suggests. Mist can enhance the appearance of this graceful and isolated, yet diminutive hill, making it difficult to gauge its height. Tinto dominates the skyline throughout Clydesdale and is very close to Clydesdale's heart. Tinto is the primary objective of this route that has a little bit of everything that is best about cycling in Clydesdale. Refreshments and warmth are provided right on cue at the cosy Tinto Hill Tea-room.

Distance: 24 miles

OS Map: Sheet 72

Terrain: It is only when crossing from one river valley to another that the cyclist has to part with some puff and even then not for long. The climb out of Kirkfieldbank, early in the route, is challenging in places. There are several moderate inclines but none are especially sustained

Short cuts: There are no short cuts that are advised but it is possible to terminate the journey early at Carstairs Junction Railway Station and take the train to Motherwell, Carluke, Glasgow or Edinburgh but not Lanark. There are two trains in the morning and one in the evening, so not very helpful. No Sunday service. Services from Carstairs are provided by several operators and they appear to be prone to regular changes, so it would be advisable to check out the situation in advance

Links: It is possible to proceed to Biggar by crossing the Boat Bridge at Thankerton, turn right at the farm as you leave Thankerton.

By the Way

It is a case of hold tight for the exhilarating downhill out of Lanark. The descent starts gently but once you have taken the left-hand turn onto the A72 it becomes steep and twisting. The view from here is a good one but it might be best to stop to take it in, as you will have to keep your eyes firmly on the road.

The downhill on the A72 into Kirkfieldbank requires care but it is not very busy and cars will not normally overtake cyclists as space is limited. A slightly more sedate alternative is to cycle straight on past the turning for the A72, on the A73 and turn left onto a quiet lane just the other side of the Cartland Bridge. Take the left-hand fork and follow the road downhill past the campsite to appear in Kirkfieldbank at the bridge over the Clyde.

Kirkfieldbank

The downhill fizzles out on the bridge across the Clyde and into Kirkfieldbank. The name describes the place perfectly, it clings to the riverbank and the kirk dominates the scene. From the bridge you can take in the 17th-century Clydesholm Bridge, the only means of crossing the Clyde at this point until 1959. Space is at a premium but there is a good range of amenities in Kirkfieldbank including a campsite, a pub, a general store, a restaurant and a play park.

Many of the homes in the village are old weavers' cottages and attempts have been made to retain the character of the village with developments mimicking the vernacular architecture.

The descent into Kirkfieldbank means a climb out of Kirkfieldbank, which is the hardest one of the trip. Once it is conquered there is a long time to recover before the next hill is tackled. High above the Clyde, you can take in the views to the south to Tinto and over to Lanark as you wind your way through classic farmland scenes on a lane intermittently lined with stone-dykes, hedgerows and beech trees.

Just beyond the large Byretown Farm there is a possible detour to the Corra Linn (highest of the Falls of Clyde), Corra Castle (ruined), Corehouse (mansion house, limited number of tours in the summer) and the Falls of Clyde Nature Reserve by continuing straight on, onto a rough un-surfaced road. Cycling is absolutely forbidden beyond the car park so your bikes would have to be left unattended.

The dead-end indicated on your left just before you turn left for Sandilands takes you to the weir, a touch up-river of the Bonnington Linn, the first of the Falls of Clyde. See Route 2 for more details of the detour to the Bonnington Linn.

The next downhill transfers you into the valley of the Douglas Water, steep towards the bottom it is necessary to restrain your momentum as a sharp right turn and a humpback bridge are waiting for you just out of sight. I frequently stop on the bridge to survey the gentle Douglas Valley and the slow Douglas Water passing beneath. An easy trip across the floor of the valley brings you to the hamlet of Sandilands. The former station cottage is wonderfully evocative of a less utilitarian age of rail travel and you can only reflect on how pleasant a journey it would have been alongside the Douglas Water.

Sandilands signals the start of the gradual ascent towards Tinto. After a brief brush with the A70 on a specially constructed 100-metre section of cycle-path you return to the quiet back roads. The country-side is now rougher, your view is restricted to the hillsides that enclose you and the farmhouses seem to have lost a storey.

Carmichael

Rolling up to the crossroads in Carmichael an old signpost points in every direction but the one you want. Straight on is the family home of the Carmichaels as is the main entrance to Carmichael Church.

The Carmichaels can boast illustrious forebears. The 2nd Lord Carmichael was a Commissioner for the Treaty of Union and the 3rd a statesman and an ambassador to Prussia, Russia and Vienna; a recently restored monument to his memory stands on Carmichael Hill.

There has been a church dedicated to St Michael in Carmichael since the 12th century. The current church was built in 1750. It has an external staircase saved from the pre-Reformation church. The church is not as austere as many that were built after the Reformation. A magnificent stained-glass window was installed in 1904, depicting figures of Noah and St Columba and the Glasgow coat-of-arms.

It is worth getting off the bike for a wander through the churchyard, when returning to the saddle you may wish to utilise the "loupin on stane" at the gate to the churchyard, a convenience for genteel ladies arriving on horseback. I am sure there are equally genteel cyclists who will be just as grateful.

The road out of Carmichael would make even the most seasoned cyclists' heart sink and contemplate returning the way they had come but thankfully we turn right just at its foot.

From Carmichael to the Tinto Hill Tea-room the road will engross the cyclist as it twists and turns and passes through farmyards (watch for livestock blocking the way), a series of crests stretch away from you as the road rises and falls. The hillsides are heathery, the air is cooler and the views into Tinto's corries are impressive.

Tinto Hill and the Tea-room

Tinto Hill was once thought to be the highest in Lanarkshire, a notion seemingly confirmed by the rhyme "Twixt Tintock Tap and Culter Fell there is just the third part of an ell" (Scots Ell = 15 in.). Culter Fell, five miles to the south-east, is unfortunately over 100 feet higher.

Mrs McIntyre's Tinto Hill Tea Room – a popular stop with cyclists

In time though Tinto may be higher as everyone who climbs it, is encouraged to carry a stone to the top and add to the huge Bronze Age cairn that surmounts Tinto. At the present rate it will be 3,500 years before Tinto reaches 2456 feet, one foot higher than Culter Fell.

The route to the summit is obvious and the erosion is testament to the popularity of the ascent. The summit can be reached in about 1 to 1½ hours. Tinto's isolated position makes it a terrific viewpoint and an indicator points out the peaks that may be visible on the horizon. On a clear day the vista extends from the Lake District to the Southern Highlands. A short distance from the walkers' car park there is an Iron Age hill fort. Circular with double ditches and ramparts it is more obvious to the descending walker.

The Tinto Hill Tea-room is situated 100 metres from the car park. This was opened in 1938 to take advantage of the boom in those searching out the great outdoors. It has a special atmosphere that is particularly appreciated by walkers and cyclists alike. In return for your custom wet clothes can be dried, water bottles filled and bladders emptied. Cyclists who come from all over ensure that the tea-room is on their itinerary and many cycling clubs have at least one visit on their annual calendars.

Thankerton

A short free-wheel from the tea-room carries us into Thankerton. Largely a dormitory village, it has the dubious pleasure of being cut in two by the main Glasgow to London railway line, but has no station. Thankerton thrived as a destination for Victorian holidaymakers with the arrival of the railway, but the Tinto Express stopped running in 1964 and the station closed shortly afterwards. Apart from good views of Tinto, there is no real reason to dwell in Thankerton. The small park is a good spot for a picnic and the village store can supply the necessary provisions.

Just beyond the turning for Biggar, by the side of the road, is a monument erected in 1911 to commemorate the arrest and execution of Donald Cargill. One of the main provocateurs in the Covenanting Movement he had a hand in "The Declaration of Sanquhar" and ex-communicated the King and other leading opponents of "The Covenant" acts which put a price on his head of 500 "Merks". Irvine of Bonshawe charged with hunting down those who held conventicles, claimed the bounty.

Covington

A gently rising road takes us through Newtown of Covington with its one remaining thatched cottage to the small but surprising collection of buildings at Covington.

The tower, built by an infamous branch of the Lindsay family, and the church date from the 15th century. The walls of the tower are 11 feet thick and surrounded by a dry moat, and within the walls there is a pit dungeon and a garderobe (toilet). The church no longer in use occupies a site that has been used for religious worship for over 1000 years. Again a wander through the churchyard is interesting for the insight into life in these parts.

Nearby is the well-preserved beehive-style dovecot built in the 16th century, it would have housed 500 pigeons. On the opposite side of the road is a cairn to commemorate the night spent here by Robert Burns on his way to Edinburgh in 1786. Burns greatly impressed his hosts as they did he. Of his host Archibald Prentice, Burns wrote, " No words can do him justice." Prentice returned the compliment by subscribing to 21 copies of the Edinburgh edition. It may have been this visit that inspired Prentice's son, as he went on to found and edit the *Manchester Times*.

Save for a couple of farms the ride to Carstairs Junction encounters very little. There are expansive views to the north and east and the cycling is undemanding.

Carstairs Junction and Carstairs Village

Some of the architecture in Carstairs Junction highlights that this is a village built by the railway companies. Once every train going to or from the south stopped here, but now there is only a couple each day. The Victorian station has been demolished and replaced by a glass and steel box. This is the point at which you may want to stop early and catch the train to either Glasgow or Edinburgh but not Lanark, avoiding the short stretch on the A70. Returning to Lanark would require a change at Carluke.

A short hop brings us to Carstairs Village. It has a rather English look to it being one of the few villages in Scotland with a village green. A handful of shops, pubs and tea-rooms are congregated round the green and this is the last opportunity for refreshment before Lanark. The whole scene is overlooked by the 17th-century Kirk that has ancient communion ware on display.

In order to complete the circle to return to Lanark the A70 is used for about one mile. The road is not generally very busy but care should be taken. Lorries carry coal to the rail depot at Ravenstruther, they do tend to give cyclists plenty of room but not if it will hold them up.

Leaving the A70 to cut through the hamlet of Cleghorn, we join the A706 at the bridge over the Mouse to return to Lanark on the most pleasant road in and out of the town.

The Route

	Grid Ref.	Miles	Details of Route
1.	886 436	0	Start: Lanark Railway Station. Leave the station car park and turn right. Go straight on at traffic lights and proceed downhill on High Street. Go through narrow gap at the foot of High Street, and continue downhill.
2.	875 438	½	Turn left onto A72, signed "Hamilton 13, Clyde Valley Tourist Route". Descend steep twisty road and cross the Clyde.
3.	868 437	¾	Take first left once over the bridge onto Riverside Road. Climb uphill for 400 metres.
4.	869 435	1	Turn left off Riverside Road at Whittingham Cottage, signed "GP Hire, Rentokil". Follow road past housing and glasshouses. Climb moderately/steeply for 1 mile.
5.	875 418	2	Surfaced road swings to right. (Straight ahead on un-surfaced road for Nature Reserve). Follow road round to right, road now tree-lined, to T-junction.
6.	874 416	2¼	At T-junction turn left onto gently descending road. Continue for almost 2 miles along dyke-lined road.
7.	884 394	4	Follow road round to right in trees. (Dead-end road for Bonnington Linn on left). Take next left signed "Sandilands 1¾" onto initially level and then fast downhill road. Restrain speed, road takes sharp right over bridge at the foot of the hill. Continue past milk tanker depot to T-junction.
8.	892 386	5½	At T-junction turn right and follow round to the left. Climb moderately past traditional red telephone box and four houses to T-junction with A70.
9.	895 379	5¾	Turn left onto cycle-path alongside the A70. After 200 metres turn right onto quiet back road, signed "Carmichael 2". Follow undulating road to T-junction at large farm.
10.	905 380	6	Turn right at T-junction and follow road to crossroads.
11.	921 384	7¾	Old signpost at crossroads. Turn right, unsigned, and proceed through Carmichael.
12.	926 380	8	Road ahead looks impossibly steep but turn right just out of Carmichael.
13.	924 364	9	Follow road round to left at dead-end signed ahead. Follow road through Lochlyvoch Farm and round the foot of Tinto Hill. Fast downhill takes you past Tinto Walkers Car Park to A73 and the Tinto Hill Tea-room.

14.	966 378	12	Go straight over A73 signed "Thankerton". Follow road gently downhill into Thankerton.
15.	973 378	12½	Just beyond bowling club turn left onto Boat Road, signed "Carstairs 6, Carnwath 7". Follow road over railway line and leave Thankerton on the downhill. Continue straight on at next right. It's uphill past Cargill Monument, through Newtown of Covington and past Covington Tower.
16.	972 405	15	½ mile beyond Covington Tower follow road round to the left and then turn right, signed "Pettinain, Cycleway". Follow road to T-junction.
17.	961 426	16½	Turn right and after ½ mile follow road round to the left at Grangehall. Beyond Grangehall climb moderately and then descend in deep cutting and cross Clyde on narrow concrete bridge and proceed into Carstairs Junction to T-junction at church.
18.	955 451	18½	Turn left and then follow road round to left past social club and continue uphill past railway station. Just beyond station turn right over railway. Follow road for about 1 mile into Carstairs Village.
19.	937 460	20	Emerge onto village green. Follow road round to left to T-junction with main road and turn left. Follow A70 out of Carstairs. Descend past Newhouse Caravan site and then climb up over railway line and into Ravenstruther.
20.	921 451	21	In Ravenstruther continue past turning for Ayr and take next right onto back road and continue into Cleghorn, take care at low and narrow railway bridge. Leave Cleghorn on downhill to traffic lights.
21.	905 452	22	Turn left onto A706 and continue along this road into Lanark.
22.	881 440	23¾	At Fire Station turn left and then take second right past Tesco. At foot of hill turn left. Go uphill. Dismount at the top of hill and push bike out onto High Street.
23.	884 436	24	Take right fork, Bannatyne Street and return to railway station.
24.	886 436	24	End: Lanark Railway Station.

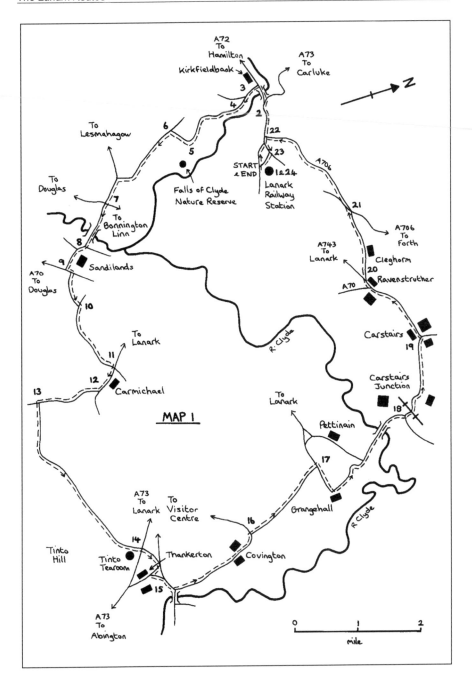

2. A Journey to Different Lands

A short ride, following the quiet dyke-lined lanes that link the small farming communities of Hawksland, Dickland and Greenrig on the high ground between the valleys of the Nethan and the Clyde. The height means good views in all directions. As it is a short ride you may want to make the short detour and walk to Bonnington Linn, the furthest upstream of the Falls of Clyde. Take a bicycle lock if you intend visiting the falls. It is just as easy to start this route from Lanark as it is from Kirkfieldbank but it is not as easy to finish in Lanark, as Lanark is about 300 feet higher than Kirkfieldbank.

Distance: 8 miles

OS Map: Sheet 72

Terrain: The first hill out Kirkfieldbank is challenging in places and if you start from Lanark you have a sustained and steep return. The trend is generally uphill on the way round but nothing more than moderate with some good downhills to compensate.

By the Way

The hill out of Kirkfieldbank gets progressively harder but it is possible to complete a circuit and avoid this hill completely, however this would depend on you finding a suitably unobtrusive spot to park beyond the hill. Alternatively the driver could deposit cyclists beyond the hill and park in Kirkfieldbank.

Once the hill is out of the way it is a relatively easy cycle along narrows lanes with extensive views over patchwork fields lined with mature broad leaf trees, a classic rural scene. The views across the deep gorge that the Clyde has carved for itself to Lanark are equally impressive. Tinto seems to loom round every bend.

As this is a short route you may want to make the one-mile detour to the Bonnington Linn, the first of the Falls of Clyde. A few hundred metres beyond the right turn for Lesmahagow there is a left turn, which is marked as a dead-end. Follow this road to the gates, secure your bikes in an unobtrusive spot, and then walk for about ten minutes to the weir that blocks the Clyde and diverts water into the hydro-system. Once at the weir walking along either bank for a short distance will reveal the complex cataract, Bonnington Linn. It is a particularly inhospitable looking waterfall. Rocks jut out and the water surges through narrow channels accentuating its power. In spate I feel they are the most intimidating of all the four Falls of Clyde. Scottish Power respectfully ask that you do not in any way interfere with their equipment and the Scottish Wildlife Trust forbid any cycling beyond the gates.

Returning to the route, you turn your back on Tinto and climb through the farming communities of Hawksland and Dickland, passing directly through farmyards. The road descends beyond the houses "Rebuilt by John Frater". Your momentum will throw you round the sharp bend at Burnside so take care.

The road ascends again through Greenhill Farm and past the listed Georgian farmhouse at Greenrig. You stop climbing just as the road turns sharp right and a superb view opens up all the way down the Clyde Valley to Glasgow, Cowal, the Campsies and the Southern Highlands. In the near distance is the National Trust property of Blackhill, crowned by an Iron Age fort. A very fast downhill takes us into a dip overlooked by a distinctive building that may have been a mill. The downhill soon resumes and whisks you into Kirkfieldbank but high hedges restrict your vision, so don't get carried away.

Bonnington Linn, the first of the four Falls of Clyde

The Route

Grid Ref.	Miles	Details of Route
1. 863 438	0	Start: Car Park Kirkfieldbank. Turn right out of car park and proceed through Kirkfieldbank.
2. 868 437	¼	Turn right onto Riverside Road just before bridge over Clyde. (If coming from Lanark turn left immediately after crossing Clyde). Follow Riverside Road uphill for 400metres.
3. 869 435	½	Take left fork at Whittingham Cottage just as road leaves Kirkfieldbank. Follow road up moderate/steep hill. Not far beyond Byretown Farm follow road round to the right at cottages and ascend to T-junction. (Straight on for Nature Reserve).
4. 873 416	2	Turn left and follow pleasant dyke lined road for ¾ mile.
5. 878 398	3¼	Take the next right, road hooks round, signed Lesmahagow. Follow undulating road past "Green Pastures" to T-junction just beyond Birkhill Farm. (Continue straight on for 400 metres for left turn for Bonnington Linn).
6. 855 395	4	Turn right at T-junction. (Road to left closed). Follow road uphill past former Hawksland Primary School and wind through farmyard to T-junction.
7. 848 399	4½	Turn right and pass row of houses rebuilt by "John Frater in 1911".
8. 850 403	4¾	100 metres beyond houses road forks take left fork and descend fairly quickly past water board site. Road turns sharply to the left at Burnside Nursery and then climbs moderately past Greenhill Farm.
9. 856 424	6¼	Road swings sharply to right. Good viewpoint. Fast descent takes you into a dip. Momentum carries you out of dip at unusual house to T-junction.
10. 865 427	6¾	Turn left and continue for 100m to T-junction.
11. 866 427		Turn left and follow road round to the right at Newhouse Farm and descend into Kirkfieldbank and follow Riverside Road to T-junction with A72.
12. 868 437	7¾	At T-junction turn left and return to car park. (Turn right for Lanark but follow the directions from Kirkfieldbank to Lanark given in Douglas to Lanark, Route 5).
13. 864 438	8	End: Car park Kirkfieldbank.

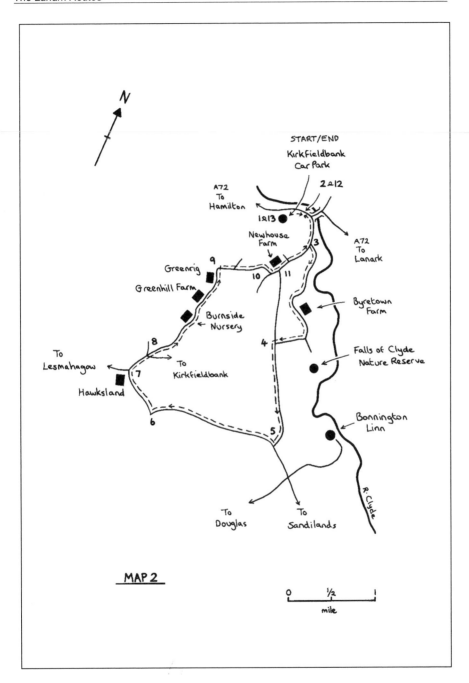

3. Four Valleys

*Visiting four valleys only means one thing, many ups and downs. It
starts easily enough with a long descent into the Lee Valley, only to
have to climb out of it onto a high ridge of land separating the Lee
from the Clyde. However the views to the Southern Highlands and
Argyll are sufficient reward. We then plunge to Crossford by the
Clyde where we have three choices, all involving climbs. The
climbs between Crossford and Craignethan Castle are especially
challenging and the downhills require restraint.*

Distance: via Craignethan Castle, 18 miles; Via Yieldshields, 15½ miles;
Lanark to Carluke Railway Station, 8 miles

OS Maps: Sheets 72, 71 and 64 (all three maps are required at one time for a
tiny section of this ride, very confusing).

Terrain: This is a ride for fit cyclists. The steep climb out of Crossford, is
quickly followed by a steeper climb out of the Nethan Valley. Pushing is an
option but with 18 miles and four steep climbs it might take all day. The alter-
natives offer more moderate gradients. The climb from Crossford to Braidwood is sustained. There is only one short steep section en route to Carluke
Station that can be tackled on foot.

Short Cuts: The best way to shorten this route is to proceed to Carluke. It is
possible to cut out Craignethan Castle, Kirkmuirhill and Auchenheath by going straight on at the top of the first climb out of Crossford, crossing the B7086
and turning left at the next crossroads to rejoin the route to Kirkfieldbank.

Links: It is only one mile or so from Kirkmuirhill to Lesmahagow. Continue
straight on from Kirkmuirhill on the B7078 to Lesmahagow where you can
start the ride to Strathaven (Route 14).

By the Way

A long moderate descent out of Lanark pauses slightly, as should you,
on Cartland Bridge. Designed by Thomas Telford, it spans the Mouse
(pronounced *moose*) in three arches, 125 ft below. Legend has it that
Wallace hid in a cave in the side of the gorge. It is not advised to attempt
to find the cave. The downhill continues pleasantly through light
woodland and sweeps past an impressive lodge that serves the private
Lee Castle. A moderate climb out of the Lee valley is tempered by the
fact that it is on a pleasing hedge-lined lane.

Nemphlar

Nemphlar, a former weaving hamlet, sits on a high spur of land that separates the Clyde and Lee valleys. Just beyond Nemphlar, on the crest of this spur, the views are impressive in all directions; be sure to look back to Lanark and Tinto beyond. The Clyde Walkway that will link Lanark with Glasgow can be accessed from Nemphlar at the Stonebyres Falls, the last of the Falls of Clyde.

Crossford

Crossford is on the floor of the Clyde Valley and we enter it by a long downhill that becomes very steep and twisting in its final stages. The red roof tiles that can be spotted through the trees are the cue to put the brakes on. Despite the name there is no need to get your feet wet, instead we cross the Clyde into Crossford on a fine 18th-century bridge. Just before crossing the bridge take a left turn for the Clyde Valley Country Estate with its wide range of visitor facilities. Glasshouses house a tea-room and a garden centre. Craft and speciality shops occupy a former stable yard as well as a restaurant. For children there is pony trekking and in the summer an old world fairground.

Fruit has been grown in the Clyde Valley possibly since Roman times. Merlin sang about the orchards of the Clyde in the sixth century and the Venerable Bede mentions them in an eighth-century verse. Crossford was once at the centre of a thriving soft fruit and tomato industry but is now largely just a pleasant commuter village. Although strawberries are still grown, the tomato growers have collapsed under pressure from imports.

From Crossford there are three choices. You can cycle the short distance to Carluke Railway Station and travel to Lanark or Glasgow. The journey starts off easily enough as you bump along the floor of the Clyde Valley then turns steeply uphill to Carluke, it is fortunately a short enough stretch to get off and push. Not far from Carluke Station you can make a detour to the birthplace of General Roy, father of the Ordnance Survey, which is marked by a triangulation pillar.

Alternatively you can return to Lanark via Braidwood, Yieldshields and Kilncadzow (pronounced *kilcaigie*). Braidwood and Yieldshields both offer good spots for picnics. At Kilncadzow's Village Home Bakery you could buy one of their famously gigantic cakes.

Braidwood's Station Inn has a good reputation for real ales and bar meals. On the hill between Crossford and Braidwood a small detour to

Tower of Halbar offers the chance to get your breath back. It sounds a creation of Tolkien, but is in fact a medieval tower house. It may date from the 14th century but 17th century is more likely, an information board explains all. The tower is now rented out as rather atmospheric holiday accommodation.

The most demanding but also the most entertaining return is via Craignethan Castle. The climb out of Crossford is just a taste of what is to come and this may be the point at which to decide to turn back. Just as the steep climb out of Crossford is conquered, a steep descent takes you into a pretty and infrequently visited section of the Nethan Valley. This may be due to the awesome climb out of the valley, up to the hamlet of Tillietudlem. The cycle to the castle is an arduous one but it can be visited on foot via the much shorter path that leads up from the bridge over the Nethan at the north end of Crossford.

Tillietudlem and Craignethan Castle

The hamlet takes its name from Sir Walter Scott's "Old Mortality", Craignethan Castle providing the inspiration for "Tillietudlem Castle". The link grew so strong that the hamlet adopted the name. It was even rumoured that Scott contemplated the castle as his home but plumped for Abbotsford instead.

A collection of imposing towers, ruined ramparts and a deep ditch, there is enough of Craignethan Castle left to take up an hour of your time. A brief but excellent guidebook tells its story. Owned by Historic Scotland, Craignethan Castle sits on a site naturally defended by steep ravines on three sides but as the land on the other side of the ravines is higher, it was particularly vulnerable to attack by artillery. Begun in 1530 by Sir James Hamilton of Finnart, it was the last private fortress to be built in Scotland. A distinctive feature of its defences is a "caponier". Situated in the ditch that defended the weak west side, it was hoped that the ditch could be scoured by hand-gunners secure in this vaulted chamber. This "caponier" is unique in Britain.

The castle was captured and re-captured several times in a fifty-year period of military activity, but every time without a fight. This was due to the Hamilton's support for Mary Queen of Scots after her abdication in 1567 and she is known to have sheltered here in May 1568.

From Craignethan the cycling is for a time at least less demanding. Skirting the villages of Kirkmuirhill and Blackwood we descend into and climb out of the Nethan Valley again to the hamlet of Auchenheath,

Craignethan Castle

a hamlet that bears all the scars of rural depopulation with its abandoned school and Post Office.

Turning left in Auchenheath the cycling returns to delightfully peaceful lanes. The sting in the tail comes when we have to climb over the shoulder of Blackhill. At the top of this climb a footpath leads off to the summit of Blackhill owned by the National Trust for Scotland. At the summit there are the remains of an Iron Age fort and a later settlement. Expansive views are to be had in every direction.

To avoid the A72 we remain above the village of Kirkfieldbank. A very fast descent takes us into the village and again to the banks of the Clyde. The last uphill of the day is into Lanark but it is best to avoid the A72 by turning left after crossing the Clyde past the campsite and Mouse Mill and a 17th-century bridge mistakenly referred to as Roman. This way into Lanark means tackling the steep "Mouse Peth" but it is quieter and there is more room for cars to overtake on the short section of the A73 than on the A72.

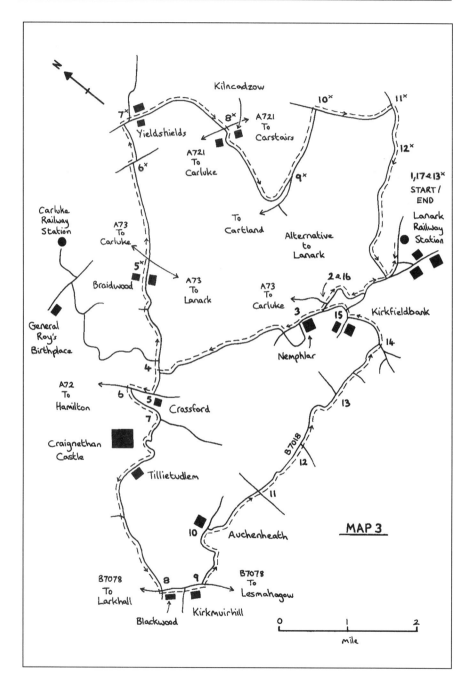

MAP 3

The Route

Lanark, Crossford and Tillietudlem

	Grid Ref.	Miles	Details of Route
1.	886 436	0	Start: Lanark Railway Station. Leave Station car park and turn right. Go straight on at traffic lights and proceed downhill on High Street. Go through narrow gap at the foot of High Street, and continue downhill out of Lanark past entrance to Cartland Bridge Hotel and over Cartland Bridge.
2.	868 445	1¼	Turn left immediately after crossing bridge. Take right-hand fork signed, "Nemphlar 1". Descend past Lee Castle Lodge and then ascend moderately into Nemphlar.
3.	856 449	2¼	In Nemphlar old signpost points the way to Crossford. Turn right and ascend for a short distance. Long straight downhill section opens up, road then turns very steeply downhill. Prepare to stop at T-junction when you spot the red roof tiles.
4.	831 466	4¼	At T-junction turn left into Crossford and cross Clyde on impressive sandstone bridge.
5.	827 465	4½	Just beyond bridge turn right at T-junction with A72 and cycle through village.
6.	824 469	5	At the dilapidated Tillietudlem Hotel turn left steeply uphill, signed "Craignethan Castle", to small group of houses.
7.	822 459	5½	Just beyond row of houses turn right signed "Craignethan Castle 1". Road descends very steeply (12%) and bottoms out at Corra Mill. Road level for a short section and then climbs just as steeply out of valley to Tillietudlem. (Entrance to Craignethan Castle on right). Hill tops out at a large brick house and swings sharply to the left. Continue past turning for Draffan. Road rises steeply then descends into Blackhill on Southfield Road.
8.	792 436	9½	At the end of Southfield Road turn left onto Carlisle Road.
9.	799 430	10	Follow Carlisle Road to junction at Kirkmuirhill Parish Church. Turn left, signed "Lanark 6, Craignethan Castle 4, Auchenheath 1", onto Lanark Road. Follow road downhill over narrow bridge and then uphill into Auchenheath.
10.	809 437	11	At crossroads in Auchenheath, just at former

			Nethanvale Coffee Shop, turn right onto Newkays Rd. Short rise out of Auchenheath, trend is generally uphill.
11.	823 431	12	Road descends for a short distance through crossroads, go straight through. Road dips and then climbs steeply past cattery and kennels to top out at Stonebyres Reservoir. Descend to T-junction with B7018.
12.	838 432	13	Turn left onto B7018 and follow downhill. Road twists through trees.
13.	852 431	13¾	At reinforced banking with barrier take narrow road that leaves on the right, unsigned. Follow rising road past traditional cottages to T- junction.
14.	867 430	15	Turn left and descend quickly into Kirkfieldbank to emerge at T-junction in village with A72. Turn right and cross Clyde.
15.	868 440	15¾	Once over Clyde take first left follow road past campsite and over old bridge and then steeply uphill turning left to arrive at T-junction with A73.
16.	868 445	16¼	Turn right and cross Cartland Bridge and ascend into Lanark following road to the top of High Street. Taking the right fork to return to railway station.
17.	886 436	18	End: Lanark Railway Station.

Crossford to Lanark via Braidwood and Yieldshields

4ˣ.	831 466	5	At T-junction, turn right. Stiff climb away from Crossford on narrow twisting road. Brief relief at Christian Healing Centre. (turn left at this point for Carluke). Continue uphill, passing by Tower of Halbar, into Braidwood, gradient relents slightly on Braidwood Main Street. Good site for picnic at small lake on right of Main Street.
5ˣ.	850 483	7	400 metres beyond lake we encounter a T-junction with the A73. Turn left and then immediately right at Station Inn onto the Boghall Road. Follow road for 1½ miles.
6ˣ.	865 499	8½	At T-junction with A721 turn right and immediately left at small industrial estate onto the Yieldshields Road. Follow road into Yieldshields and round to the right past small play park.
7ˣ.	872 507	9	Just beyond park at next T-junction turn right onto Lymes Road. Moderate downhill following course of Roman road. Road dips to burn and then climbs moderately/steeply. Road tops out at 1000 feet, again good views. Road descends quickly into Kilncadzow.
8ˣ.	884 487	10¼	At T-junction with A721 school turn left and then immediately right past Kilncadzow Village Hall. Continue descent on Craigenhall Road. Road goes through

severe "S- bend" on leaving Kilncadzow and then embarks on an even faster descent. Good visibility. Passing through a conifer forest the road turns sharply left and runs parallel to railway line.

9ˣ. 882 467   11½   Continue past turning over railway and descend for about ½ mile and then ascend moderate slope for ½ mile.

10ˣ. 901 473   12½   At T-junction at large farm, turn right. Ascend for a short distance and then follow roller coaster like road. Road takes sharp left at conifer forest. (Site of Roman Camp).

11ˣ. 912 459   12½   Turn right at T-junction onto A706 and descend over level crossing to traffic lights at narrow bridge over Mouse.

12ˣ. 905 453   13½   Turn right after crossing bridge and climb moderately following road round to the right signed "Lanark A706". Continue along this road into Lanark. Just beyond fire brigade station turn left. Take second on the right downhill past Tesco. At bottom of hill turn left. Go to top of hill and follow road round to right. Push bikes across pedestrian footpath onto High Street.

13ˣ. 886 436   15½   Take right-hand fork to return to Lanark Railway Station. End.

4. Yieldshields Circular

This is a good ride to fill a morning or afternoon that is going spare.
It takes advantage of the roads that criss-cross the high moor to the
north of Lanark, taking in the hamlets of Yieldshields, Kilncadzow
and Cartland. There are good views and an exceptional bakery at
Kilncadzow.

Distance: 15½ miles

OS Map: Sheet 72

Terrain: The initial climb is a long moderate ascent to the Harelaw roundabout. From here short inclines interspersed with long flat sections is the order of the day. The route from Yieldshields to Kilncadzow involves a
moderate/challenging climb but is followed by a very long downhill. Unfortunately there is a steep but not too long a climb into Lanark.

Short Cuts: Carluke is only one mile further on from Yieldshields, where you
catch the train to Lanark or Glasgow. It is easy to miss out Cartland but just as
easy to include it. Cartland and the Mouse Valley can be missed out alto-
gether by following the alternative return from Crossford to Lanark from
Kilncadzow. In so doing you replace a steep climb with two moderate climbs.

Links: This route almost meets Route 7. To join Route 7 at Braehead turn
right almost immediately after turning left as per point 6 in the route details.

By the Way

Departing from Lanark on elegant Hope Street we gradually gain the
high moorland that stretches to the east. The vista to the south and east
from the Harelaw roundabout is impressive, taking in the Pentland
Hills, the Broughton Heights and Culter Fell. From this point on the
route is a very peaceful affair and the cycling varied.

In places beech trees line both sides of the road, evocative of the
avenues of plane trees in France but for the most part it is exposed and
rugged moorland and the wind can cause problems. The road takes its
time linking farms in turn, eventually finding its way to the hamlet of
Yieldshields. An unremarkable but attractive hamlet, the only reason
for tarrying would be to picnic in the small park at its centre. (From
Yieldshields it is a straightforward ride into Carluke; turning right at the
park is the best way).

The ride from Yieldshields to Kilncadzow follows the course of a

Roman road. Builders of straight roads they may have been but there is nothing the Romans could do about the hills – as we find on the roller-coaster to Kilncadzow.

Kilncadzow

1,000 feet above sea level the views from Kilncadzow are impressive. Its two most notable points are; one, the unusual pronunciation of Kilncadzow, i.e. *kilcaigie*; two, the Home Bakery by the side of the A721, which serves up gargantuan cakes.

From Kilncadzow it's a fast and exhilarating downhill with good views of Tinto and Culter Fell all the way. Beyond the railway line you can make the detour through the hamlet of Cartland or continue on the long downhill into the Mouse Valley. The impressive native woodland that occupies the valley is a designated Nature Reserve and there are pleasant but informal walks through it.

After a short steep pull (it's okay to get off and push) on a narrow winding lane out of the Mouse Valley, where the visibility is poor, you will find yourself in Lanark.

A chocolate eclair that just has to be shared!

The Route

	Grid Ref.	Miles	Details of Route
1.	886 436	0	Start: Lanark Railway Station. Leave Station Car Park and turn right. Go straight on at traffic lights and proceed downhill on High St. Go through narrow gap at the foot of High St.
2.	880 437	¼	100 metres beyond narrow gap turn right, signed A706, Linlithgow and Forth. Follow road out of Lanark, to set of traffic lights 2 miles out of Lanark.
3.	905 452	2¼	At traffic lights turn left go over narrow bridge. Climb moderately to level crossing. Continue along road to roundabout.
4.	917 472	3½	At roundabout go straight ahead signed A706 Forth and Linlithgow.
5.	918 474	3½	150 metres beyond roundabout turn right onto descending narrow road. Momentum carries you up small rise lined by beech trees. Continue along level road to T-junction.
6.	936 493	5	Turn left and follow road to crossroads.
7.	923 506	6¼	Go straight over A706 onto Yieldshields Road. Follow road for 3 miles passing turning for Springfield Fishery and the equestrian centre.
8.	873 507	9½	Once in the hamlet of Yieldshields take the first left, just beyond row of prefabs, onto Lymes Road. Descend moderately to dip and then climb moderately/steeply. Road tops out at about 1000 feet. Short fast descent to T-junction with A721.
9.	884 487	10¾	Turn left and then immediately right. Descend through Kilncadzow. Leave hamlet on severe S-bend and continue to descend. Road levels out and runs parallel to railway line.
10.	883 467	12	Turn right over railway line and follow road round to the right at fork in the road. Continue parallel to railway but this time on the opposite side and going in the opposite direction. Road swings away from railway line and enters hamlet of Cartland.
11.	866 462	13¼	In Cartland follow road round to left and ascend away from Cartland. Road tops out at the large Greentowers Farm. Road descends gently at first. At modern bungalow, road becomes very steep.
12.	876 455	14	Just beyond bungalow turn right downhill. Very fast and twisting downhill takes you over the Mouse. Steep climb up other side of valley on narrow road. Poor visibility.

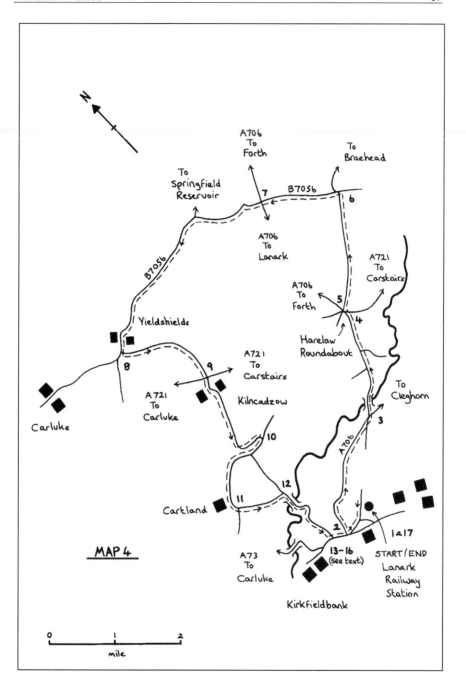

N

A706
To
Forth

To
Braehead

To
Springfield
Reservoir

B7056

7

6

B7056

A706
To
Lanark

A721
To
Carstairs

Yieldshields

A706
To
Forth

5

4

8

9

A721
To
Carstairs

Harelaw
Roundabout

A721
To
Carluke

Kilncadzow

To
Cleghorn

3

Carluke

10

A706

12

11

Cartland

MAP 4

2

1 & 17

13-16
(see text)

A73
To
Carluke

START / END
Lanark
Railway
Station

Kirkfieldbank

0   1   2

mile

13.	877 442	15	At top of hill turn left onto Wheatlandside and climb gently through housing. Go straight over at crossroads to T-junction at top of hill.
14.	882 443	15¼	Turn right and after 30m turn right again. Follow for about 100 metres to Fire Station.
15.	881 440	15¼	At Fire Station turn left and then take second right past Tesco. At foot of hill turn left. Go uphill. Dismount at the top of hill and push bike out onto High Street.
16.	884 436	15½	Take right fork, Bannatyne Street and return to railway station.
17.	886 436	15½	End: Lanark Railway Station.

5. Crusaders and Covenanters

This is a route for confident cyclists. To complete it, the A70 has to be followed for about a mile (five if you choose to visit Douglas) as does the A73 for 1½ miles south of Roberton; these sections are not especially busy. There are two high passes and terrific views on offer. There is a long section of cycle-path and the cycling in the Douglas Valley is just delightful.

St Bride's Church in Douglas contains the embalmed heart of "Good Sir James" who promised his friend Robert the Bruce to take his heart to the Holy Land to fight in the Crusades. His 14th-century tomb and those of his descendants are also within the church. One of the effigies adorning a tomb is vivid to say the least.

Douglas has played a prominent part in Scotland's history. Like the rest of Clydesdale it supported the Covenanters.

Distance: Lanark to Douglas 24½ miles; Douglas to Lanark 12½ miles

OS Map: Sheet 72

Terrain: The two high passes follow each other in quick succession. The first requires a bit more effort as it climbs in stages through 500 feet from the floor of the Douglas Valley. Puffing and panting is only required in the final push to the top. The second pass comes out higher but is a surprisingly gentle ascent. There are two short steep sections between the A73 and the cycle path. The final climb into Lanark is also a strenuous one.

Links: From the point where you turn off the A73 it is only 1½ miles to Abington. A good long ride is to form a figure-of-eight with the Abington to Wanlockhead ride, Route 18, "God's Treasure House in Scotland".

By the Way

As you leave Lanark on Hyndford Road all its credentials as a county town are on display. First is the Livestock Market, the focus for most of the rural county, if there is a market being held, it is easy enough to pull over and have a peek. Next is the rather dilapidated racecourse, races have been held here since 1160. The imposing tote is now listed. The impressive "Silver Bell" was awarded annually, the earliest known winner was in 1628, until 1979 when racing ceased. Right at the end of the racecourse is the unmistakably militaristic architecture of the

Winston Barracks, opened just before World War II. Long since abandoned, they have an uncertain fate.

Hyndford Bridge transfers you across the Clyde, and it has done this job since 1773. The low building facing you as you cross is the tollhouse. Unfortunately it is necessary to cycle along the A70. After about one mile you leave it for a delightful lane that carries you along the Douglas Valley. A poem on the wall of a farm, the first you will encounter in the Douglas Valley gives good advice, look back as you pass to see it.

Be ye man
Or be ye wummin
Be ye gaun or be ye comin
Be ye in rags or be ye in lace
Tak yer time
Slow doon yer pace

Not far beyond the tiny hamlet of Sandilands, the first significant climb of the day gets underway. From about 600 feet by the banks of the Douglas Water you climb to 1100 feet over a distance of three miles. Only in the latter stages does it become tough. What a view! Tinto is immediately to the left, hang-gliders and parapenters are a common sight as are birds of prey, Culter Fell dominates the view in the mid distance and the Lowther Hills are just beyond on the right, with their distinctive "golf-ball" radar domes.

A very fast downhill leads you into the long settled and lush valley of the Garf Water and to the foot of your next climb. A very gradual climb takes you again above 1000 feet, on the shoulder of the not much higher Dungavel Hill, the view is expansive and there is a real feeling of emptiness. The exhilarating downhill takes you over the Nap Bridge and into Roberton. A tiny but very bonnie hamlet, so take your time or you will miss it.

The second necessary evil of the day is 1½ miles on the A73, which can be busy on weekdays. We return to the back-roads at Maidencots to tackle a climb local cyclists refer to as "The Staircase". If cyclists give a climb a name then it is sure to be a tough one.

Traffic ceases to be a problem at all, when you join the cycle-path that runs parallel to the B7078. The constant gradient can be rather tedious but your eyes will be free to take in the huge expanse of high moor that surrounds you.

The Clyde and the Hyndford Bridge

Douglas

At the end of the cycle-path you can make a detour to the village of Douglas. The centre of Douglas is a tight network of narrow streets that set an ancient tone. A wander along these narrow streets will reveal a rich history. On Main Street there is a memorial cairn to James Gavin, the tailor and Covenanter whose ears were cut off, by Claverhouse, with his own shears and banished to Barbados. The lintel that he carved above his door is incorporated in the memorial.

St. Bride's Church, with its 17th-century octagonal tower, houses what is thought to be the oldest working clock in Scotland. Presented to the church by Mary Queen of Scot's in 1565, it chimes three-minutes ahead of each hour in the spirit of the Douglas motto "Never Behind". A sign on the gate will tell you where to obtain the key to the church. Through glass, set in the floor of the church, can be seen the casket that contains the heart of "The Good" Sir James Douglas, one of Robert the Bruce's right-hand men in the fight with England. He promised Bruce he would take his heart to the Holy Land to compensate for Bruce's unfulfilled desire to fight in a crusade. Sir James was killed in Spain in

1330 at the hands of the Moors, en route to the Holy Land. His time worn tomb and that of other Douglases line the walls.

Side by side with the heart of Sir James is the heart of Archibald Douglas, who died in 1513. A beautifully carved and slightly spooky marble effigy of Lucy Elizabeth, Countess of Home, on a black marble base sits on the altar. Two old battle tattered Cameronian regimental flags hang in the church. The Cameronian regiment started life as the Angus Regiment. Not far from St Bride's is a statue of their founder the Earl of Angus pointing to the field where the regiment was raised in 1689.

Overlooking the churchyard is the oldest intact building in Douglas, built in 1621, it started out as the courtroom and prison, for a time it was the Sun Inn; currently, it is a private house.

The Douglas Heritage Museum, which concentrates on the Cameronians and the area's mining heritage, is adjacent to St Bride's Church. Converted to a school in 1706, the building is immediately recognisable by its traditional architecture.

The Douglas Estate, to the east of the village, is the grounds of the demolished Douglas Castle. At the entrance to the estate, on the right, is a modest memorial to the Polish Calvary Regiment, whose headquarters in exile during World War II was Douglas. A tiny remnant of the old castle remains, which many believe is "Castle Dangerous", the subject of Scott's last novel of the same name. Not far from the ruined tower is a cairn that commemorates the disbanding of the Cameronian regiment in 1969.

As there is much to see in Douglas, it will mean a long stop in the village and you may wish to take the opportunity to obtain refreshments. There is a café to the rear of the petrol station on the Ayr Road and a bakery that provides hot snacks to take away. Unfortunately no-one seems to be offering bar meals.

The return to Lanark is via a delightful lane along the opposite side of the Douglas Valley from the one you left on. You can maximise the pleasant cycling by continuing to Kirkfieldbank but this means a big climb into Lanark. To avoid this you can return via Sandilands and the route by which you left Lanark.

The Route

Lanark to Douglas

	Grid Ref.	Miles	Details of Route
1.	886 436	0	Start: Lanark Railway Station. Leave station car park and turn left. Proceed to T-junction just beyond entrance to Cattle Market.
2.	887 433	¼	Turn left signed A73, Carlisle. Follow Hyndford Road. passing Lanark Loch, the racecourse and the barracks. Short downhill brings us to traffic lights.
3.	914 414	2	Traffic lights regulate traffic over Hyndford Bridge once over bridge turn right signed Ayr, A70. Follow A70 uphill for 1 mile.
4.	904 400	3	Just as A70 narrows to a single lane turn right onto narrow lane. Follow road running parallel to Clyde. At the hamlet of Sandilands follow road round to the left.
5.	892 384	4½	Turn right at red telephone box. Road climbs gently away form the Douglas Water to T-junction opposite low cottage.
6.	881 358	6½	Turn left and cycle short distance to T-junction with A70.
7.	885 354	6¾	Go straight over A70, signed "B7055, Wiston 5½". Follow road uphill past Rigside Water Reserve. Just over 1 mile of moderate climbing brings you to the top of the hill. A very fast descent takes us into the Garf Valley.
8.	925 331	9½	Control speed and prepare to make right-hand turn at white cottage at the foot of the hill, signed "Roberton 3". Climb steadily over 1000 feet summit of pass. Fast descent to Roberton. Cycle through Roberton to T-junction with A73
9.	946 286	12¾	Turn right onto A73 Follow A73 for 1½ miles.
10.	935 262	14¼	Just beyond junction of A73 and A702 turn right. Road rises and then falls going under M74. Climb moderately/steeply up to junction with B7078 and cycle-path.
11.	901 253	16½	Cross B7078 and turn right onto cycle-path on far side. Cycle-path makes long steady ascent past the Red Moss Hotel. Cycle-path becomes cycle lane and then descends to T-junction with A70. Cycle lane ends.
12.	855 326	22	Turn left and follow A70 for 2 miles into Douglas.
13.	835 309	24	End: Douglas, St Bride's Church

Douglas to Lanark

	Grid Ref.	Miles	Details of Route
1ˣ.	835 309	0	Start: Main Street, St Bride's Church. Follow Main Street away from the village centre onto Colonels Entry and follow uphill out of Douglas to junction with A70 opposite the hospital, turn left.
2ˣ.	856 327	2	At first roundabout go straight through, signed "Lanark, Coalburn, Services".
3ˣ.	859 330		At second roundabout turn left, signed "Glasgow B7078".
4ˣ.	855 334	2½	500 metres from roundabout turn right through gap in central reservation onto minor road. Signed "Douglas Water 3". Short climb brings us to gently undulating road through woodland. Follow road until short climb brings you to T-junction.
5ˣ.	867 364	4½	Turn right. Follow this road all the way to Kirkfieldbank ignoring all side roads but go round to the left when straight on is indicated as a dead-end. Also follow road round to the right at Newhouse Farm for downhill into Kirkfieldbank.
6ˣ.	868 439	11	Hill runs out at T-junction in Kirkfieldbank with A72 turn right and cross River Clyde.
7ˣ.	868 440		Take left immediately after bridge and follow road past campsite and over bridge short steep climb brings you to entrance of large house take right opposite entrance and follow narrow road to T-junction with A73.
8ˣ.	868 445	11½	Turn right onto A73 and follow into Lanark. Once in Lanark proceed to traffic lights at the top of High Street.
9ˣ.	884 436	12½	Take right fork for Bannatyne Street and cycle short distance to Lanark Railway Station.
10ˣ.	886 436	12½	End: Lanark Railway Station

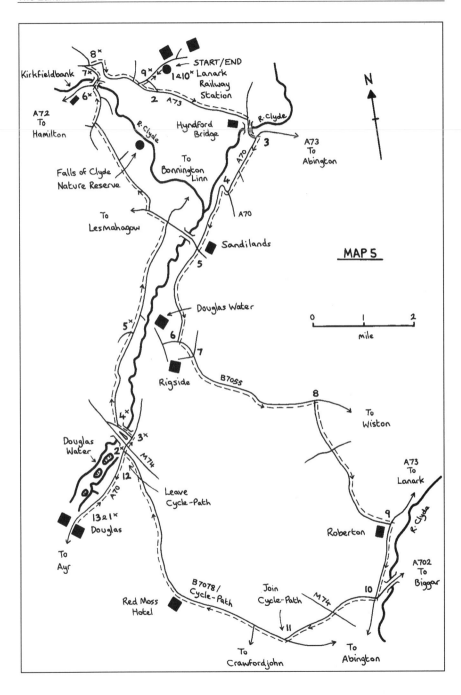

MAP 5

6. A Journey to Scotland's Centre

Like "Route 5" this ride also links two historic burghs, Lanark being a Royal Burgh and Carnwath a subordinate in its role as a burgh of barony. Carnwath is an understated and intriguing village with many buildings in the vernacular architecture. Carnwath is also the place furthest from the sea in Scotland. Pettinain is a pretty hamlet with a long ecclesiastical history.

Distance: Lanark to Carnwath 8 miles; Carnwath to Lanark 9¼ miles

OS Map: Sheet 72

Terrain: A long moderate climb out of Lanark is followed by a mainly level cycle to Carnwath. There are only really two other climbs, which are short and not too steep but noticeable nonetheless.

Links: A Biggar to Carnwath route is described in the Biggar chapter (Route 13), which could be combined with this route to create a Lanark to Biggar ride.

By the Way

The first three miles take you to the high point of the day of 800 feet at the Harelaw roundabout. We lose very little of this height on our way to Carnwath.

We encounter very little in the way of settlement in this empty area of high moorland rather it is the landscape that offers interest. Closer to Carnwath hundreds of tiny hillocks have bubbled up on the surface. These are in fact 'kames', piles of moraine that were deposited by retreating glaciers. Many of the local place names reflect their proximity to these kames such as Kames Country Club and Kaimend. These huge piles of sand and gravel enabled the early development of golf in this area, as conditions are similar to those found on links courses.

All of a sudden the landscape changes to a bleak moonscape of exposed peat. Riven with drainage ditches and surrounded by a narrow gauge railway, this is a peat extraction works. If you find yourself here at the weekend it can be quite eerie looking out over the silent expanse of skinless earth.

A very short stint on the A70 through Carnwath golf course is necessary. On the left a well-defined motte is clearly visible from the road.

Looking east to The Pentlands

Carnwath

Carnwath comes as a bit of a surprise. The first building of note that we encounter is the St Mary's Aisle, on the right-hand side of the road, adjacent to the parish church. The well-preserved remnant of a larger collegiate church built in 1424. The vaulted roof is covered with stone slabs making it the second oldest building in Scotland with its original roof. Inside the recumbent figures of Hugh, Lord Sommerville (d. 1549) and his wife Janet (d. 1550) adorn their tombs. A plaque to the rear of St Mary's Aisle commemorates some prominent local Covenanters. The key to St Mary's Aisle can be obtained from the Lee and Carnwath Estate Office immediately adjacent on the right.

Main Street Carnwath is a continuous line of cottages and villas some with crow-stepped gables, a deliberate attempt to make Carnwath look bigger than it actually is and deter attackers. Most of the existing buildings are Victorian, which gives Carnwath a very sober air.

A notable exception is the Wee Bush Inn, dating from 1750, which is still thatched. The name is thought to have been acquired from Robert

Burns' motto "Better a Wee Bush than nae Bield" (bield = shelter). Robert Burns is known to have spent two nights here in 1786.

Carnwath is the furthest point from the sea in Scotland and therefore it is a very cold place in winter (lowest recorded temperature: -26.6°C). Carnwath was considered in earlier times a difficult place to reach. Regular visitor James IV described the journey from Edinburgh as a "Lang Whang" (a long way). The 17th-century Mercat Cross that stands on the Main Street also acts as a mileage indicator and gives the distances to each coast. Grave robbers Burke and Hare are said to have exploited Carnwath's isolated position by hiding out here whenever the heat was on in Edinburgh.

Carnwath's final claim to fame is that it hosts, in August, what is thought to be the oldest foot race in Scotland the Red Hose Race, inaugurated in 1508. The winner is awarded a pair of red socks by the local laird.

It is necessary to cycle out of Carnwath again on the A70 but you leave it after a short distance to cycle past the rather intimidating Carstairs State Hospital, a high security establishment for the criminally insane. After a brief spell in Carstairs Junction it is over the Clyde and into open country again.

Pettinain

It is not long before you encounter the small but pretty hamlet of Pettinain. The church dates from the 17th century but there is known to have been a priest at Pettinain in 1147. A pleasant half an hour can be spent wandering in the churchyard, if only to appreciate the surprisingly good view from this well-defined promontory.

A short fast downhill sweeps you away from Pettinain. A moderate climb follows but an even faster downhill carries you all the way to the A73 and onwards to the 18th century, and still in very good order, Hyndford Bridge. A final uphill draws you level with the now abandoned Winston Barracks, with its unmistakable military architecture, and the dilapidated racecourse with its monolithic tote. Both give some idea of Lanark's fall from grace.

The Route

Lanark to Carnwath

	Grid Ref.	Miles	Details of Route
1.	886 436	0	Start: Lanark Railway Station. Leave Station Car Park and turn right. Go straight on at traffic lights and proceed downhill on High Street. Go through narrow gap at the foot of High Street.
2.	880 434	¼	100 metres beyond narrow gap turn right, signed "A706, Linlithgow, Forth". Follow road out of Lanark, to set of traffic lights 2 miles out of Lanark.
3.	905 452	2¼	At traffic lights turn left go over narrow bridge. Climb moderately to level crossing. Continue along road to roundabout.
4.	917 472	3½	At roundabout go straight ahead signed "A706, Forth, Linlithgow".
5.	918 474		150 metres beyond roundabout turn right onto descending narrow road. Momentum carries you up small rise at section lined by beech trees. Continue along now level road to T-junction.
6.	936 493	5	Turn right. Follow level road, crossing small bridge at Shodshill Mill. Just beyond bungalows you roll up to T-junction.
7.	945 490	6¼	Turn right follow level road over brick bridge.
8.	947 481	6¾	Take left 900 metres beyond brick bridge and follow still level road past peat extraction works and small lochs to arrive at T-junction with B7016.
9.	966 472	8¼	Turn right and proceed past cemetery to arrive at T-junction with A70.
10.	968 467	8½	Turn left over railway bridge and cycle short distance into Carnwath.
11.	978 464	9	End: Carnwath Mercat Cross, half way up Main St.

Carnwath to Lanark

	Grid Ref.	Miles	Details of Route
1.	978 464	0	Start: Carnwath Mercat Cross. With your back to the Mercat Cross turn left downhill on Main Street and leave Carnwath passing golf course.
2.	964 466	1	Just out of Carnwath, at West End turn left signed "Carstairs State Hospital". Follow road through small village and past entrance to CSH. Go under one railway and over another on the Lampits Road into Carstairs Junction.

3. 956 450   2½   Take first left in Carstairs Junction, at church and War Memorial. Signed "Pettinain 2, Cycleway". Leave Carstairs Junction on the downhill and cross Clyde on narrow concrete bridge. Climb moderately in deep cutting.

4. 963 437   3½   At top of hill turn right, signed "Pettinain ½". Ascend gently into Pettinain. Short steep descent out of Pettinain.

5. 951 425   4½   At bottom of hill take right-hand fork and then turn right at T-junction, signed "Lanark 5". Ascend gently through trees. Fast downhill carries you to junction with A73.

6. 926 414   6½   Turn right onto A73 and follow for ½ mile to traffic lights.

7. 915 414   7   Turn right at traffic lights over Hyndford Bridge. Moderate ascent past Winston Barracks and then level road past racecourse into Lanark.

8. 887 434   9   At livestock market turn right and return to railway station past supermarket.

9. 886 436   9¼   End: Lanark Railway Station.

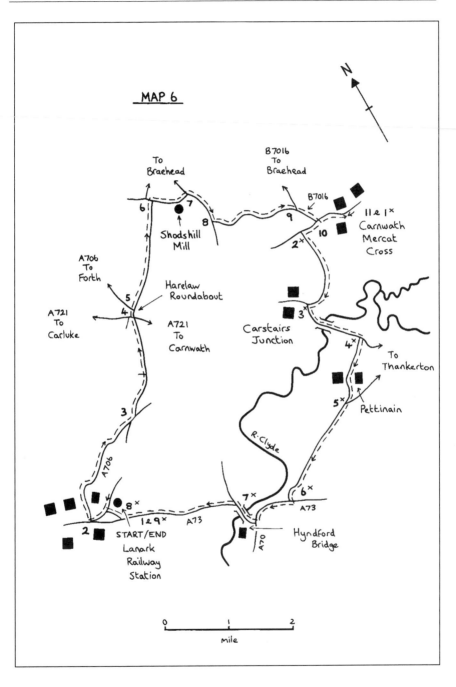

7. Go to Forth and Cycle

*This is a forgotten corner of Clydesdale, but it was at the vanguard
of the Industrial Revolution in Scotland. There is much evidence of
its industrial past with railway and mining paraphernalia lining
the way. Pleasant and interesting countryside surround Forth.
Auchengray is a product of the golden age of rural living and
Braehead is an engaging legacy of the mining era.*

Distance: 14½ miles

OS Map: Sheet 72

Terrain: A short climb to Auchengray and a climb past Ampherlaw House
neither climb is particularly difficult. Mostly the route is pleasantly undulating.

Getting there

Road

From the south: leave the M74 at junction 12 and follow A70 for Lanark,
turning left over the Hyndford Bridge. Proceed through Lanark and turn
right beyond High Street onto A706 signed Forth and Linlithgow, follow all
the way to Forth. *From the north and west:* leave the A8/M8 at junction 6,
follow A73 for Lanark and Peebles. At Carluke follow the A721 for
Peebles turning left onto the A706 at the Harelaw Roundabout 5 miles out
of Carluke. *From the east:* follow the A71 out of Edinburgh following either
the A704 or A706 beyond West Calder.

Rail

Nearest stations are Lanark 8 miles and Shotts (Dykehead) 6 miles (Glasgow to Edinburgh via Bellshill Line). See Links Routes Chapter.

Links: This route could be joined with Route 4 to form a figure-of-eight as the
two routes come within one mile of each other to the south-west of Braehead.
Turn right almost immediately after turning left as per point 6 Route 4. This is
the best way to cycle from Lanark to Forth.

By the Way

Cycling out of Forth on Manse Road gives ample opportunity to take in
the view that would otherwise be obscured by Main Street. The view
stretches out over the high moors to the Pentland Hills and serves to
exemplify Forth's high and exposed position.

   There had to be a good reason for people to settle in such large
numbers in such a bleak locality. The reason, except for Auchengray,

was coal. The Mansewood Hotel and Colliery Restaurant, one of the first buildings after leaving Forth, displays old coal wagons, emphasising the mining heritage. It also boasts a first class children's play park for patrons and could be an alternative starting point.

Wilsontown

Not far out of Forth you will come across the factory village of Wilsontown, which was built to house the people who flooded in to work in the iron works. The Wilson brothers founded the village and works in 1779, attracted by the locally available coal, limestone and ironstone. They established what were the first iron works in Lanarkshire and only the second in Scotland. So successful were the works that by 1812 over 2000 people lived in the village. A church, a school and bakery were built to serve the population in this otherwise empty landscape. 1812 was the beginning of the end for Wilsontown as the costs of transportation and internecine squabbling brought litigation and bankruptcy. The works were rarely in service after 1812, finally closed in 1824 and erased from the landscape in 1974. Today Wilsontown is a quiet village and all that remains are the track beds, spoil heaps and the grass-grown foundations. Going between the piles of a dismantled railway bridge you can wander amongst what remains. The moors have a bleak and wild beauty and the cyclist can feel very much alone travelling out to Haywood and beyond to Auchengray.

Haywood

Haywood is barely recognisable today as a settlement, but it was once a mining village of 1200 inhabitants with all the amenities of a thriving community including a railway station served by a branch line of the Caledonian Railway. The ruin overlooking the scene, was once the hotel. On a windowsill there is a carved lament to the desolation, addressed to Annie a former landlady:

O Annie wert thou here tae see, A waefu (woeful) wummin thou wad be.

Auchengray

After probably the most significant climb of the route you will encounter the small rural community of Auchengray. The row of cottages sits back from the road, as they replace earlier thatched dwellings that remained until the new houses were built in the 19th century. A once-thriving rural community, the row of cottages housed a joiner/undertaker, a Post Office, a pub and a smithy. Between them the joiner and the blacksmith built Auchengray carts. All that remains is the Auchengray Inn, a welcoming and cosy hostelry, its open fire providing the perfect antidote to a cold day. Inside there is railway paraphernalia saved from the now demolished Auchengray Station.

Along from the village centre is a particularly distinctive church. The façade facing the road was designed by 'Modern Gothic" architect F.T. Pilkington in the style of a Coptic church in Alexandria, Egypt.

Beyond Auchengray the countryside is pleasantly engaging and not at all bleak. A ruined church amidst swaying corn and a small humpbacked bridge conjure a particularly picturesque scene at Fordmouth. The mansion house at Ampherlaw and the ancient tower at Eastshields, point to a long legacy of prosperous farming.

Braehead

We avoid the direct route into Braehead. Instead, a loop takes us through this isolated community. It was here that the Cameronian Minister John MacMillan was based in Braehead between 1743 and 1753, erecting a presbytery in August 1743.

The Last Shift Inn

Braehead is unmistakably a mining village. The Last Shift Inn is the strongest link in the village with its mining past, the equivalent of the 19th hole for weary miners; open for meals at the weekend and children are welcome in the lounge.

A fast descent out of Braehead means a moderate climb towards Wilsontown. A short cut into Forth involves fording a small burn (footbridge alternative). The romance of the ford though is tempered by the steep climb into Forth.

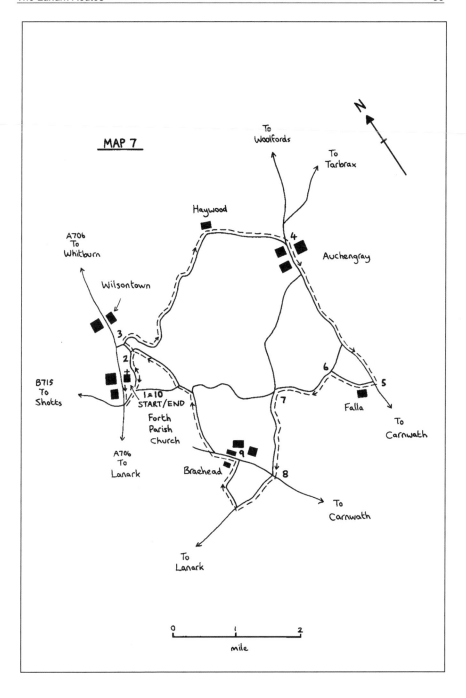

The Route

Grid Ref.	Miles	Details of Route
1. 942 538	0	Start: Kirk, Forth Main Street.
		With your back to the church turn left. After 50 metres turn left onto Manse Road. Follow road past the Bowling Club and recreation ground. Eventually arrive at a fork in the road at disused church.
2. 949 546	1	Take left fork past Mansewood Hotel. Just beyond hotel turn right, signed "Haywood 2, Auchengray 4".
3. 948 548	1¼	Turn right again almost immediately and enter Wilsontown on the downhill. Follow road round to the left out of Wilsontown. Pass by open cast colliery. Road dog-legs at Haywood. Follow road over railway line and then uphill to T-junction at Auchengray
4. 996 543	5	Turn right into Auchengray. Proceed through Auchengray and leave on a fast downhill. Follow road to the left when road swings to the right. Follow undulating road. Continue past turning for "Pat Baxter Furniture".
5. 994 503	7½	Take next right after "PB Furniture" through small group of houses in trees. Ascend past entrance to Ampherlaw House.
6. 987 511	8	Follow road round to the left over railway bridge. Continue over sandstone bridge and then uphill to T-junction.
7. 973 516	9	Turn left. Follow intermittently tree-lined road to staggered crossroads at Eastshields Tower.
8. 959 501	10¼	Turn left and then right. Follow road for about 1 mile taking the first right encountered just opposite Scabgill Farm. Follow road into Braehead and proceed along Main Street to T-junction opposite Last Shift Inn.
9. 955 508	11¼	Turn left. Leave Braehead on the downhill. Continue along this road following signs for "Wilsontown, B7016". Eventually arriving back at the cemetery and disused church. Turn left and return into Forth on Manse Road.
10. 942 538	14½	End: Kirk, Forth Main St.

The Biggar Routes

Biggar Background

Biggar is an open and inviting town that nestles on a high plain between the Clyde and the Tweed. Its wide medieval High Street bristles with activity and curiosities. For a town that was made a burgh of barony in 1451 it seems peculiarly vulnerable to attack but perhaps congeniality was its defence. Several Scottish sovereigns are known to have enjoyed hunting in this area staying at Boghall Castle.

The feudal Lords of Biggar were the Flemings. The Flemings occupied Boghall Castle and were responsible for the founding of the towns St Mary's Collegiate Church in 1545, the last to be built in Scotland prior to the Reformation. A Fleming daughter, Mary, was selected to accompany the young Mary, Queen of Scots to France in 1548. At the annual Biggar Gala Day a local girl is crowned the Fleming Queen.

Biggar is a town that takes its heritage seriously. Five museums are to be found and all but one is maintained and run by the voluntary Biggar Museum Trust, which is also responsible for Brownsbank Cottage at Candy Mill (the last home of Hugh MacDiarmid) and the John Buchan Centre in Broughton. The five museums are as follows:

Moat Park Heritage Centre: a display of models that illustrates Clydesdale's geological formation and its Roman and Iron Age heritage. Housed in a former Kirk it also contains the impressive 'Moffat Menzies' tapestry.

Gladstone Court: a hands-on museum that recreates the 19th century. A Victorian street with small shops and a schoolroom are part of the experience.

The Albion Museum and Archive: the Albion Motor Company was started with a bond on a local farm. The museum exploits this link and has a few vintage Albion vehicles on display and it houses the Albion Archive.

Greenhill Covenanters' House: this 17th-century house was built in its original location during 'The Killing Times', a bloody period when people who supported the National Covenant were hunted down for worshipping on the open moors rather than be subjected to the state-controlled religion. Heroically saved and moved by the Biggar Museum Trust from a site eight miles away near Tinto it takes the visitor back to these times displaying a copy of the National Covenant and other Covenanting artefacts.

Gasworks Museum (National Museums of Scotland): built in 1839 the Biggar Gasworks are the only preserved gasworks in Scotland.

An attraction that will be a big hit with younger cyclists is the **Biggar Puppet Theatre**; housed in a complete Victorian theatre in miniature, it puts on shows most days.

Greenhill Covenanters' House

Practical Information

Getting There

Road: From Edinburgh: follow the A702 from the centre of Edinburgh for 29 miles. From Glasgow: leave the southbound M74 at junction 7, Larkhall and Lanark (Clyde Valley Tourist Route) and follow the A72 via Lanark and Symington. From the south: leave the M74 northbound at junction 13, Abington and follow the A73 north and then the A702(T) for 12 miles via Lamington and Coulter.

Rail: The nearest railway stations are Lanark and Carstairs Junction. Follow Route 1 from Lanark to Thankerton, turning left over the Boat Bridge as you leave Thankerton for Biggar; from Carstairs Junction follow Route 13.

The village green at Skirling

Eating and Drinking

This is a visitor-oriented town and there are many establishments offering refreshment. The Elphinstone Arms, The Clydesdale Inn and The Crown are all on the High Street and offer bar meals. There are several cafés, chip shops and restaurants, but worthy of special mention is the Coffee Spot on the High Street providing excellent home baking and a warm welcome. The Church of Scotland provides a cheap and cheerful option in the Gillespie Centre also on the High Street. Many large mansion houses surrounding Biggar have been converted to country hotels they provide good meals in grand surroundings but are not especially expensive.

Staying

There is plenty of accommodation on offer in Biggar and the surrounding area but the only offering at the budget end is the campsite within Biggar Park next to the small boating pond and golf course. The local tourist information office provides a free accommodation booking service and can be contacted on (01899) 221066.

8. Into the Pentlands and the "Raspberry Republic"

A ride that ascends out of Biggar into the Pentland Hills, you cycle to the head of an infrequently travelled valley to the hamlet of Dunsyre, a hot bed of Covenanting activity. On the return journey you can cross the "border" into the "Raspberry Republic" and visit Little Sparta, the celebrated concrete poetry garden of Dr. Ian Hamilton Finlay.

Distance: 20 miles

OS Maps: Sheet 72

Terrain: This route starts with a long gradual climb, which levels out in places. The loop in the Pentlands should not pose too many problems. Save for a couple of rises, the trend is downhill. A hill blocks the return to Biggar, which involves an ascent of over 300 feet in a relatively short distance.

Links: Extend this trip by joining Route 12 at point 2, adding 5½ miles.

By the Way

You begin by climbing out of Biggar, bending round the ancient St Mary's Kirk. The general trend continues gently uphill, cutting across pleasant farmland and skirting large old farms, stalwarts of Clydesdale's farming heritage.

Once across the A721 you will begin to get the feel of the Pentland Hills that stretch to the edge of Edinburgh. The Black Mount rises to your right as you pass through a succession of small groups of houses that claim some association with the hamlet of Walston.

Walston

At the foot of the Black Mount sits the tiny hamlet of Walston proper. An interesting church and churchyard sit out on a limb and can be reached by descending a steep gravel drive on the left just before the red telephone box.

The church dates from the 17th century when the "Baillie" aisle was added to an earlier but now demolished church. In the churchyard there are a couple of good examples of portrait headstones dating from the early 18th century.

Peaceful Pentland cycling

From Walston the trend is generally downhill. Raising your eyes to the skyline on the left you can take in the rounded heads of the Pentland Hills. Not very high but the concentration of summits gives them the feel of a mini mountain range, indeed the "Pentland Poet" Allan Ramsay referred to them as "tow'ring taps".

A dark tunnel of overhanging trees leads you past Newholm, once the home of Covenanter Major Learmouth. Learmouth was the commander of the horsemen in the battle fought on nearby Rullion Green in 1666 where the Covenanters were roundly beaten by the forces of Colonel Tam Dalyell. A wanted man, Learmouth would elude his pursuers via a passage from Newholm to the banks of the Medwin.

Dunsyre

We enter Dunsyre through the piles of a dismantled railway bridge. Nowadays it is hard to believe that places such as Dunsyre were connected to the railway network. Dunsyre Church can be clearly spotted as you approach, it can be accessed from a lane that passes in front of a row of low cottages. The current church with its crenellated bell tower occupies a perfectly peaceful spot. It dates from the 19th century although the churchyard is much older. William Somervil, a former minister who was a signatory to the National Covenant of 1638, is buried here. A set of 'jougs' – the Scottish equivalent of English stocks – is to be found in the wall behind glass; the use of these was a humiliating and uncomfortable punishment for behaviour deemed unacceptable by the Church. They were placed around the neck and set at such a height in the wall so that the wearer could neither stand nor sit.

The church is no longer in use but it is usually open. Inside on a window ledge is a bell dated 1578 and an information sheet tells the story of how a local shepherd Adam Sanderson tried to help a dying Covenanter injured at the battle of Rullion Green. The Covenanter was anxious to see the Ayrshire Hills one last time. He died before this was possible but the shepherd Sanderson buried him on Black Law (4 miles north of Dunsyre) from where you can make out the Ayrshire Hills, a touching accommodation. The original marker stone also sits on the windowsill.

One mile beyond Dunsyre opposite a small patch of conifer trees a sign points the way to Lanark Road, Stonypath and Little Sparta. Stonypath is the home of poet Dr. Ian Hamilton Finlay and Little Sparta is the remarkable garden in which his poetry is expressed in concrete form. The garden provides a very particular environment for each of his poems, which include Nuclear Sail and Air Craft Carrier Bird Table. A visit to Little Sparta is only possible mid June to September, Friday and Sunday afternoons.

Newbigging

A gradual uphill is followed by a very relaxing approach to the village of Newbigging. Newbigging may strike you as unusual as it does not seem to huddle together like other Scottish villages in such an exposed location. The Nestlers Hotel offers the only opportunity for food and drink on this route.

On the left as you make your way through the village is a distinctly pagan-looking Mercat Cross. Dated 1693, it is believed to have been left behind while on its way from Dolphinton to Skirling.

The return to Biggar involves a short downhill section on the A721, which you leave for a steep climb to over 1000 feet, though the countryside regains a hospitable aspect. Near the top an old signpost points to East Gladstone, once home to close relatives of the Victorian Prime Minister. From here an almost uninterrupted free-wheel returns you to Biggar.

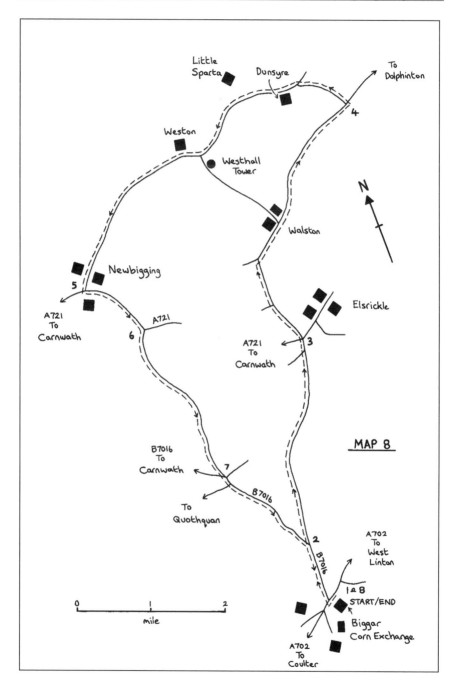

Little
Sparta ■

Dunsyre ■

To
Dalphinton

4

Weston ■

Westhall
Tower ●

N

Walston ■■

Newbigging ■
5 ■

Elsrickle ■■

A721
To
Carnwath

A721

6

A721
To
Carnwath

3

MAP 8

B7016
To
Carnwath

7

B7016

To
Quothquan

2

A702
To
West
Linton

B7016

1 & 8
START/END

Biggar
Corn Exchange ■

A702
To
Coulter

0   1   2
mile

The Route

	Grid Ref.	Miles	Details of Route
1.	043 379	0	Start: Biggar Corn Exchange. Turn left onto High Street, after 100 metres or so turn right, signed "Carnwath B7016" and climb past Moat Park Heritage Centre out of Biggar.
2.	041 390	1	Road forks ahead. Take right-hand fork, signed "Elsrickle 3". Follow undulating road to crossroads with A721
3.	055 430	4	Go straight over A721 continue past school and follow road round to the right at the next junction. Proceed through Walston on a gentle downhill.
4.	083 472	8	At the next junction in the trees turn left signed "Dunsyre 1". Follow road through trees over bridge. Short uphill through piles of dismantled railway bridge brings you to Dunsyre. Follow this road all the way to Newbigging. ("Little Sparta" on right).
5.	014 458	13½	At T-junction with A721 turn left. Follow A721 downhill for about 1 mile.
6.	023 446	14½	When road bends to the left and conifer trees line both sides of the road turn right, signed "Biggar 4 ½". Long uphill takes you over 1000feet. Steep and fast descent brings you to T-junction with B71016.
7.	028 410	16½	Turn left onto B7016 and follow into Biggar, turning left at T-junction with High Street, to return to Corn Exchange.
8.	043 379	19	End: Biggar Corn Exchange

9. Through the Biggar Gap to Broughton

A short ride through perfectly beautiful countryside, that takes us out of Clydesdale and into Tweeddale to visit the typical Borders village of Broughton, reputedly the resting place of King Arthur's magician Merlin.

Distance: 12¼ miles

OS Map: Sheet 72

Terrain: You will only notice a couple of inclines one on the way there and one on the way back. In the main the cycling is relaxed.

Links: This route can be combined with route 10 from point 4, to extend this route by one mile. It also adds a big climb to over 1000 feet.

By the Way

On the journey away from Biggar the countryside seems to take on a whole new quality. The fields are of deep green, the hills rise gently and the road undulates gracefully. Navigation is simple, a minimum number of turns and a sense of direction is maintained as you can see Biggar or Broughton or both for much of the time. All in all this is a very relaxing day.

Broughton

Broughton seems to come too soon but a short detour to the left just before entering the village leads to the old churchyard. A plaque at the entrance explains that St Llolan or St Maurice may have established a church here as early as the 7th century. A vaulted chamber attached to the sole remaining wall of the church has been rather optimistically declared as St Llolan's cell. The key can be obtained from the village shop.

The village is idyllic, it is just as a village should be. On your left at the T-junction with the Main Street is a private garden that becomes a spectacular floral display in summer, on the right is the Laurel Tea Rooms.

Broughton claims to have associations with King Arthur and Merlin. Close inspection of the OS Map will reveal names such as Merlindale the reputed resting place of the poet/magician (grave marked by a tree) and Altarstone the spot where St Kentigern is said to have baptised

Cardon Hill (2194 ft) and Culter Fell (2430 ft)

Merlin. Merlin may have lived and died here but John Buchan, author of the "The Thirty-nine Steps" definitely holidayed here. Buchan is best known for classic adventure tales, and when you take in the landscape that surrounds Broughton you cannot fail to agree with the villagers that it must have in some way inspired him.

The Buchan Centre, to the south of the village beyond the turning for Coulter, is largely devoted to the life of the author but also includes some local history. The Buchans still have a house in the village.

Cycling towards the Buchan Centre you may have noticed the Greenmantle Brewery, which brews a collection of real ales such as "Greenmantle" (a Buchan novel) and "Merlin's Ale". Unfortunately there is no local pub at which to sample the ales, so you will have to look out for them elsewhere.

The return to Biggar is just as delightful as the outward leg but the road that skirts Goseland Hill is narrower and more peaceful than the B7016.

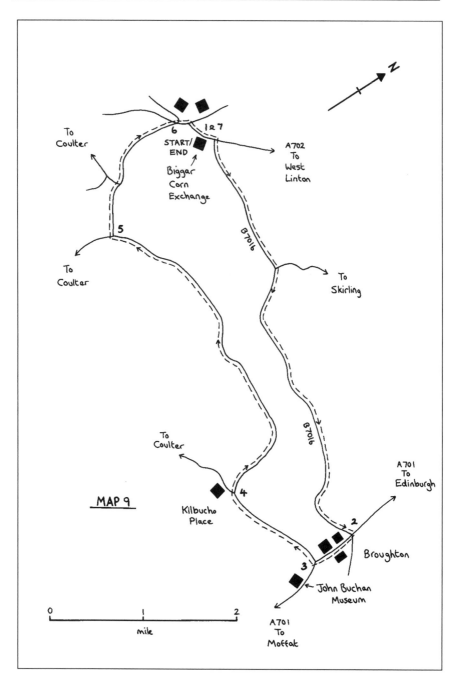

To Coulter

6
START/ END

1 2 7

A702
To
West
Linton

Biggar
Corn
Exchange

5

To
Coulter

B7016

To
Skirling

B7016

To
Coulter

MAP 9

Kilbucho
Place

4

A701
To
Edinburgh

2

Broughton

3

John Buchan
Museum

0   1   2
mile

A701
To
Moffat

The Route

	Grid Ref.	Miles	Details of Route
1.	043 379	0	Start: Biggar Corn Exchange. Turn right along High Street after 300 metres turn right, signed "Broughton B7016". Short climb out of Biggar. Follow road all the way to T-junction with Broughton Main Street.
2.	113 367	5	Turn right, signed "Moffat A701" and proceed along Broughton Main Street.
3.	113 359	5½	Just beyond Greenmantle Brewery cross Biggar Water and dismantled railway. Take next left, hooks back on itself, signed "Culter 6, Hartree 5½, Tweed Cycleway". Follow road to fork at Kilbucho Place.
4.	096 353	6½	Take right fork signed "Hartree 5" follow undulating road.
5.	048 357	10	Road climbs steeply but just before you reach the top of the hill turn right signed "Biggar 1½". Fast downhill leads you past the Hartree House Hotel. Road levels out and enters Biggar.
6.	038 376	12	At T-junction, at the end of Station Road, with Biggar High Street, turn right to return to Corn Exchange.
7.	043 379	12¼	End: Biggar Corn Exchange.

10. Kilbucho Circular

A complete circle of Goseland Hill, that involves a big climb out of the valley of the Kilbucho Burn, a discrete valley that would appear to have been an iron-age metropolis. There are fine views of Culter Fell and Cardon Hill.

Distance: 12¼ miles

OS Map: Sheet 72

Terrain: This a route for those of you who are looking for a climb. The climb out of the Kilbucho valley is a demanding one but the views will make it worthwhile.

Links: This route can act as an extension to route 9.

By the Way

The first landmark you catch sight of on leaving Biggar on Station Road is Boghall Castle. Twice besieged and taken, firstly by the Regent Moray in 1568 and secondly by Cromwell in 1650, precious little of it remains. James VI and his mother Mary Queen of Scots came to stay for peaceful and recreational reasons.

In the trees you pass the impressive but welcoming Hartree House Hotel. A short steep uphill is compensated by a long gentle downhill with just the occasional rise all the way to Kilbucho, accompanied by the Biggar Water.

Two large mansion houses take the name Kilbucho and stand more or less at the entrance to this innocuous valley but its dog-leg configuration hides the sting in the tail.

Once over the humpbacked bridge the climb starts and its full extent is revealed. Climbing to over 1000 feet you find yourself not far below the surrounding hill tops. The best views however are short of the summit of the pass.

From high on the hillside, it is easy to pick out the mounds that mark the forts and settlements in the middle distance on Mitchell Hill. Further up the wide glaciated valley are Nisbet and Snaip where half a dozen forts and settlements litter isolated hillocks, which were perfect for the purpose.

Coulter Kirk

Coulter

Mature deciduous trees line the descent into the village of Coulter, a pleasant little village with a disproportionate number of mansion houses in and around it.

The church, with its back to you, is the first building on your right as you enter the village. The round churchyard suggests that it predates the church by a considerable margin; possibly seven or eight hundred years. Anthony Murray, a prominent Covenanter, is buried in the precinct of this attractive church, as is the Victorian kleptomaniac Adam Sim. Sim built up a large collection of all things antiquarian, some suggest by doubtful means. Most were donated to the National Museums of Scotland but some still litter the ground around his home at Coulter Mains (private).

The corn-mill in Coulter has been converted to a restaurant of some repute and a 19th-century library sits opposite, a facility that is not afforded nowadays.

You need to back track for a short distance to find the return to Biggar. Pleasant, if bumpy, hedgerow-lined lanes return you to Hartree House Hotel from where the route into Biggar should be familiar.

The Route

	Grid Ref.	Miles	Details of Route
1.	043 379	0	Start: Biggar Corn Exchange. Turn left onto High Street and follow High Street to Cadgers Brig and War Memorial.
2.	038 376	¼	At War memorial turn left onto Station Road. Leave Biggar on Station Road and continue past entrance to Hartree House Hotel. Ascend short stiff climb to T-junction.
3.	048 357	2	Turn left, signed "Broughton". Road descends quickly and then undulates along the valley of the Biggar Water. Road then swings away from Biggar Water.
4.	096 353	5½	Just beyond Kilbucho Mains Farm turn right signed "Coulter 5". Proceed past Kilbucho Place and follow rising road, steep in places, to summit of pass at 1100 feet. (Continue past right for Biggar and downhill into Coulter).
5.	032 343	10	To return to Biggar take right ¼ mile short of Coulter. Road swings to the right after short downhill at East Mains. Follow gently rising road (rough surface), going round to the left at Thripland Farm to T-junction.
6.	040 361	11	Turn right at T-junction and follow to second T-junction.
7.	042 362	12	Turn left and follow road into Biggar, turning right at the end of Station Road to return to Corn Exchange.
8.	043 379	12¼	End: Biggar Corn Exchange.

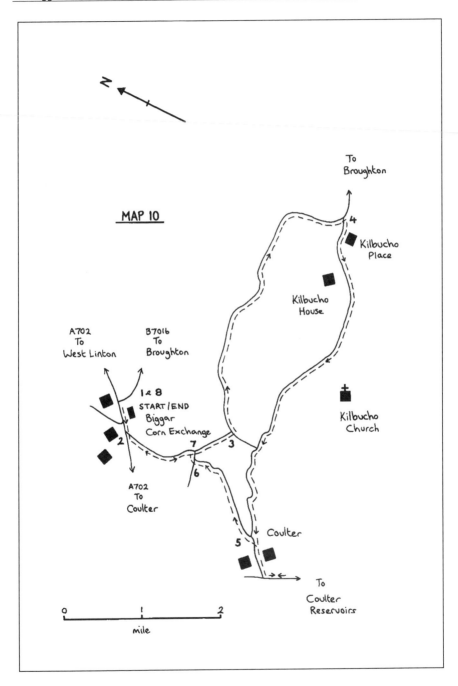

11. Skirling, Candy Mill and Elsrickle

A little piece of England, the last home of one of Scotland's foremost poets and the exposed hamlet of Elsrickle all combine to produce a very entertaining cycle.

Distance: 11 miles

OS Map: Sheet 72

Terrain: There are several small climbs but nothing horrendous. The cycling from Elsrickle to Biggar is particularly gentle.

Links: Extend this trip by joining Route 12 at point 2, adding 5½ miles.

By the Way

This ride starts as if Broughton-bound, following for a short time the Biggar Water on its way to join the Tweed. The signpost welcomes us to Scottish Borders but we refuse the invitation and turn left onto a quiet lane that leads to the hamlet of Skirling with a distinctively English feel to it.

Skirling

A large village green dotted with broad-leaved trees is surrounded by pretty cottages and picturesquely overlooked by the village kirk. In one corner is Skirling House, designed by Ramsay Traquair, the Arts and Crafts architect, for Lord Carmichael in 1908, it now provides unique and intimate accommodation to discerning travellers. At the opposite end of the green is the Douglas Davies Gallery. Occupying a former coaching inn (18th century), it displays Davies' almost abstract land-scapes and seascapes. A short uphill leads you out of Skirling, but on the downhill that follows control your speed if you want to avoid ford-ing the burn at its foot. There is no warning of the impending ford.

Candy Mill and Brownsbank Cottage

Taking the first opportunity to leave the A702 leads you above Candy Mill, but the next right will take you down to the hamlet. Just beyond the hamlet, reached by a short section of Roman road is Brownsbank Cottage. Home to the poet Hugh MacDairmid (Christopher Grieve) from 1952 until his death in 1978, it is now maintained by the Biggar Museum Trust who have returned the cottage to the way MacDairmid

Candy Burn ford

left it. MacDairmid's best known work is the poem "A Drunk Man looks at the Thistle". The cottage is home to South Lanarkshire's writer in residence and so visits are by appointment only, contact Biggar Museum Trust on (01899) 221050.

On the way to Elsrickle, by the side of the road, is the ruined Edmonston High House. This may have been a home of the 4th Earl of Morton, Regent to the young James VI, who is said to have introduced the guillotine to Scotland and the first to test its function. Further down the drive is the castellated mansion house, Edmonston House (private).

The stark silhouette of Elsrickle is your goal on the skyline, the red telephone box seems alien to the scene. Once you have climbed up to Elsrickle, the kirk stands to your left with its back to the prevailing wind. As there is not much shelter, you will probably be glad to lose height and follow a little used road through the gentler valley of the upper reaches of the Biggar Burn, with Tinto looming on the horizon.

The B7016 returns you to Biggar but you may want to extend your trip by adding The Round of Biggar Common.

The Route

	Grid Ref.	Miles	Details of Route
1.	043 379	0	Start: Biggar Corn Exchange. Turn right along High St. After 300 metres turn right signed Broughton, Public Park and Puppet Theatre and ascend short uphill and out of Biggar into open country.
2.	068 378	1½	1 mile out of Biggar, descend fairly quickly. At bottom of hill turn left signed Skirling ¾ mile onto narrow lane. Follow road past large houses to T-junction with A72.
3.	074 388	2¼	Turn right onto A72 and cycle through village of Skirling to the large War Memorial on traffic island.
4.	076 393	2½	Turn left at War Memorial and ascend out of Skirling. Road eventually turns steeply downhill to Candy Burn. Ford burn; cobbled surface. No warning but there is a footbridge. Short climb to A702.
5.	065 033	3½	Turn right onto A702. Remain on A702 for ½ mile. Leave A702 at next left unsigned. Climb moderately above Candy Mill. Road levels out, then descends quickly and then rises again to T-junction with A721 at Elsrickle.
6.	059 432	5½	Turn left onto A721. After ¼ mile and take next left.
7.	054 428	6	Road descends quickly but be ready to turn right. DO NOT RIDE TO BOTTOM OF HILL. Follow level road for 2 miles to T-junction.
8.	029 410	8	Turn left onto B7016 and follow road all the way into Biggar. Turning left at T-junction with Biggar High Street to return to Corn Exchange.
9.	043 379	11	End: Biggar Corn Exchange.

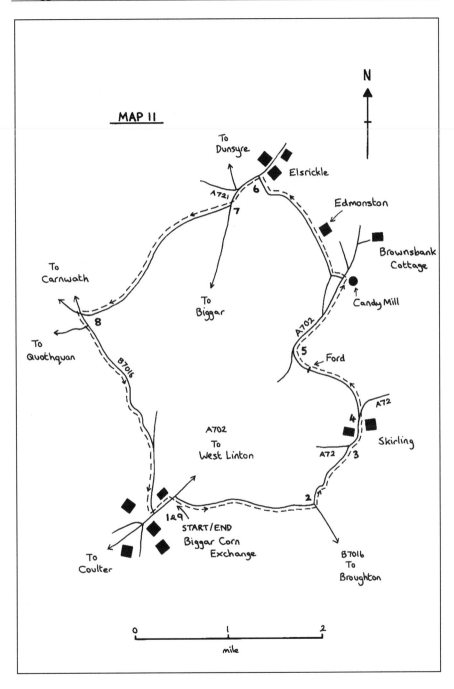

MAP 11

To
Dunsyre

Elsrickle

6

A721

7

Edmonston

Brownsbank
Cottage

To
Carnwath

To
Biggar

Candy Mill

8

A702

To
Quothquan

B7016

5   Ford

A72

4

Skirling

A72   3

A702
To
West Linton

2

129

START/END
Biggar Corn
Exchange

B7016
To
Broughton

To
Coulter

N

0   1   2

mile

12. The Round of Biggar Common

This is a short, pleasant cycle around an extended area, to the north west of Biggar, known as Biggar Common. On the way you pass through the agricultural hamlet of Quothquan and you can visit a motte by the side of the road at Wolfclyde.

Distance: 10 miles

OS Map: Sheet 72

Terrain: A long gradual climb leads you away from the Clyde and over at Cormiston. This is the gentler side of the hill and the climb is followed by a very fast downhill. Taking the left-hand fork at Quothquan will half the amount of ascent required. A large part of this route is level.

Links: An extension to routes 8 &11which join this route at point 2.

By the Way

A northerly departure from Biggar necessitates a climb but it is not too demanding. Two miles out of Biggar on the B7016 you may be able to catch a glimpse, depending on the foliage, of Carwood an imposing but ruined mansion house which had associations with the Gladstone family.

The B7016 is left for a delightfully sheltered and level road. At one point the trees overhang to create a darkened tunnel but specs of light penetrate to dapple the road. It is on this stretch that you pass the Shieldhill Hotel. Once the home of the Chancellors who inhabited the old tower after their mansion house was burned down for supporting Mary Queen of Scots in 1528 at the Battle of Langside. Its transformation to a mansion house took place in the 18th century. It is now a hotel of some repute especially for its food. The isolated position of the hotel has attracted the likes of Nelson Mandela.

Quothquan

Just beyond the hotel you encounter the hamlet of Quothquan. Quothquan never seems to come to a focus as it is strung out along one side of the road. At the far side the road forks and an old signpost points the way. Beyond the right-hand fork you will be able to see the gable end, with a bell tower and its bell still in situ, of Quothquan Kirk. The Chancellors are buried in the church aisle. Some of the tombstones

The half bridge 'Boat Bridge'

make interesting reading, they highlight the part played by local people in the British Empire and their adventurous spirit.

The descent from Quothquan to the Clyde is a fast one. Thankerton sits on the far side reached by the peculiar-looking half bridge, known as Boat Bridge, built in 1778 to replace the ferry.

With Tinto to your right, the incline that takes you away from the Clyde gradually reveals Culter Fell to the south.

If you allow the very fast downhill to carry you straight on for 200 metres, rather than turn left for Biggar as directed, you can surmount Culter Motte Hill. The motte is maintained by Historic Scotland and an information board tells of its likely origins and occupants. At first it seems an unlikely site for a defensive installation but once on top of the motte you can appreciate the uninterrupted view up and down the Clyde and through to the Tweed.

Backtrack the 200 metres or so for the turning for Biggar for an easy return on a level road.

The Route

	Grid Ref.	Miles	Details of Route
1.	043 379	0	Start: Biggar Corn Exchange. Turn left onto High Street, after 100 metres or so turn right, signed "Carnwath B7016" and climb past Moat Park Heritage Centre out of Biggar.
2.	029 408	2	Two miles out of Biggar. Take the first left signed "Thankerton 5½, Quothquan 3½", onto Shieldhill Road. Follow level and shaded road past Shieldhill Hotel into the hamlet of Quothquan.
3.	995 395	4	Road forks at far end of hamlet at telephone box. Take right fork. Road descends very quickly to the level of the Clyde to T-junction.
4.	981 382	5¼	At T-junction turn left, signed "Biggar 4". Road climbs steadily uphill dipping at small group of houses at Cormiston. From Cormiston road descends steeply.
5.	018 366	8	Just as the hill runs out turn left signed Cycleway. Straight and level road returns you to Biggar. Turn left at T-junction with High Street to return to Corn Exchange. (Continue Straight on for Culter Motte Hill).
6.	043 379	10	End: Biggar Corn Exchange.

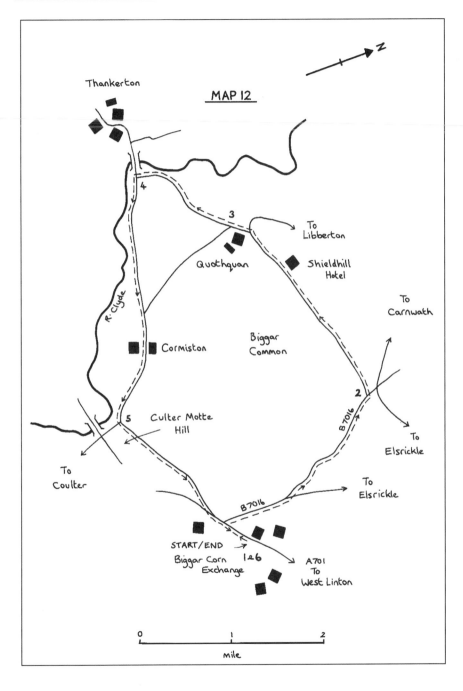

Thankerton

MAP 12

4

3

To
Libberton

Quothquan

Shieldhill
Hotel

To
Carnwath

R. Clyde

Biggar
Common

Cormiston

2

B7016

To
Elsrickle

5 Culter Motte
Hill

To
Coulter

To
Elsrickle

B7016

START/END
Biggar Corn
Exchange

1 & 6

A701
To
West Linton

0   1   2
mile

13. Biggar to Carnwath and back again

From one historic burgh to another, on the way out you take the high road to the right of the Clyde returning by the gentler low road on the opposite bank.

Distance: Biggar to Carnwath 8 miles; Carnwath to Biggar 12½ miles

OS Map: Sheet 72

Terrain: Carnwath is higher than Biggar. Inevitably there are hills to be tackled, two in particular stand out. Early in the route the climb to Cormiston attracts a rating of 10% but it is short enough for you to get off and push. The other is just short of Carnwath, a very steep section gets the climb from the Medwin Water off to a difficult start but it does not last long. The return involves the other side of the hill at Cormiston but it is longer and more gradual. This route isn't all hills and there are long undemanding sections.

Links: Link this route with Carnwath to Lanark for a Biggar to Lanark ride.

By the Way

This route borrows from many other rides already described in this guide. It is included because it is still a worthwhile ride should you be based in Biggar or Carnwath. The only section unique to this route is the section from Quothquan to Carnwath via Libberton.

Libberton

The hamlet of Libberton stands at 700 feet, its steepled church built in 1812 dominates the scene. The kirk seems far too grand for such a small community but Libberton parish encompassed Carnwath until 1137, so it is a parish with a long history and undoubtedly considers itself a prominent one. Ancestors of the Victorian Prime Minister William Gladstone are buried in the churchyard.

The following places are listed in the order in which you will encounter them from Biggar to Carnwath and back again, with the page reference adjacent. The directions for this route are given to avoid confusion and constant page flicking.

Quothquan (Route 12, page 78), Carnwath (Route 6, page 47), Carstairs Junction (Route 1, page 18), Pettinain (Route 6, page 48), Covington (Route 1, page 17), Thankerton (Route 1, page 17) and Culter Motte Hill (Route 12, page 79).

The Route

Biggar to Carnwath

	Grid Ref.	Miles	Details of Route
1.	043 379	0	Start: Biggar Corn Exchange. Turn left onto High Street, take second right, at Cadgers Brig and War Memorial. Follow road round to the left up "The Wynd" to T-junction.
2.	038 376	¼	Turn left onto Lindsaylands Road. Follow road out of Biggar along long straight and level road to T-junction.
3.	018 366	1½	Turn right onto Cormiston Road. Ascend hill (10%). Road tops out at Cormiston House. Road rises and dips and then rises into trees.
4.	003 376	2¼	At junction in trees turn right, unsigned. Road ascends gently into elongated hamlet of Quothquan.
5.	996 398	3½	At red telephone box turn right through Quothquan.
6.	996 397		100 metres further at Eastertown Farm turn left, signed "Carnwath 4¼, Libberton 2¼". Sharp right follows short sharp downhill. Road then gently rises to T-junction with B7016.
7.	994 427	5½	Turn left signed "Carnwath 2¾, Lanark 9¼". Short uphill takes you into Libberton. Downhill out of Libberton road bottoms out at River Medwyn. Road climbs away from Medwyn, steeply for a time. Shortly you will arrive at traffic lights in Carnwath.
8.	979 464	8	Turn left to find yourself at Carnwath Mercat Cross.
9.	979 464	8	End: Carnwath Mercat Cross

Carnwath to Biggar

	Grid Ref.	Miles	Details of Route
1*.	978 464	0	Start: Carnwath Mercat Cross. With your back to the Mercat Cross turn left downhill on Main Street and leave Carnwath passing through golf course.
2*.	964 467	1	Just out of Carnwath, at West End turn left signed "Carstairs State Hospital". Follow road through small village and past entrance to CSH. Go under one railway and over another on the Lampits Road into Carstairs Junction.
3*.	955 450	2½	Take first left in Carstairs Junction, at church and War Memorial, signed "Pettinain 2, Cycleway". Leave Carstairs Junction on the downhill and cross Clyde on narrow concrete bridge. Climb moderately in deep

cutting. Continue straight on at the top of the hill signed "Cycleway".

4*.   968 427   5   Fast downhill brings you to a right turn at Grangehall/Southholm Boarding Kennels, signed "Thankerton 3½, Cycleway".

5*.   961 426   5½   Not much further on take next left at old signpost onto Covington Road, signed "Thankerton 3, Cycleway". Follow to T-junction.

6*.   972 405   6¾   Turn left, signed "Thankerton, Cycleway". Follow road round to the right and continue past Covington Mains and through Newtown of Covington.

7*.   978 383   8¼   Road dips to bridge over small burn after short climb out of dip turn left at farm signed "Biggar 4, Tweed Cycleway, Carnwath 6, Quothquan 1½", and cross Clyde on impressive sandstone bridge. Follow this road steadily uphill and then after small dip and rise, go fast and steep downhill.

8*.   018 366   11¼   Just as the hill runs out turn left signed "Cycleway". Straight and level road returns you to Biggar. Turn left at T-junction with High Street to return to Corn Exchange.

9*.   043 379   12½   End: Biggar Corn Exchange.

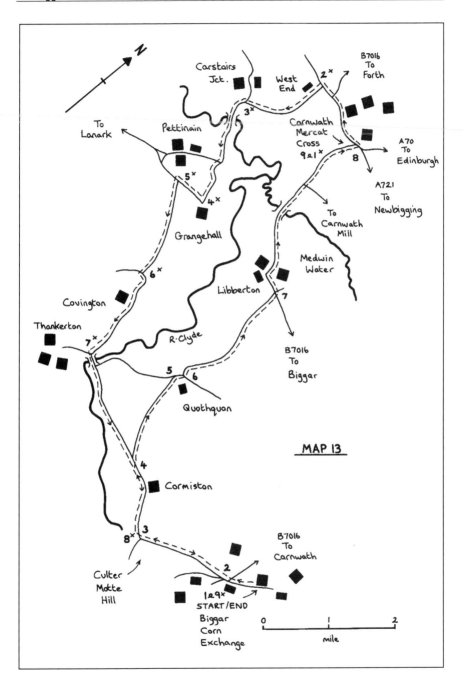

Carstairs
Jct.

West
End

B7016
To
Forth

2

To
Lanark

Pettinain

Carnwath
Mercat
Cross
9 & 1

A70
To
Edinburgh

8

A721
To
Newbigging

3

5

4

To
Carnwath
Mill

Grangehall

Medwin
Water

6

Libberton

7

Covington

R. Clyde

Thankerton

7

B7016
To
Biggar

5   6

Quothquan

MAP 13

4   Cormiston

8   3

Culter
Motte
Hill

B7016
To
Carnwath

2

1 & 9
START/END
Biggar
Corn
Exchange

0   1   2

mile

The Strathaven Routes

Strathaven Background

The Common Green is at the heart of this attractive and bustling town. High in amenities and slightly quaint it has long been a popular place to live for commuters working in Glasgow. Music hall entertainer Sir Harry Lauder set up home here.

Strathaven has always been an enterprising community. It is well known for its own brand of gingerbread and toffee. The "Strathaven Toffee" pioneers, the Gilmours, still trade on the Common Green. For a long time it was the mills that provided employment and the town tried very hard to sustain the industry, moving from woollens to linen then to cotton and finally to silk, but to no avail.

Tightly wound streets make it difficult to get a sense of the place but a wander is worthwhile and will reveal craft shops, artisan bakers and other curiosities. The mock Tudor and the "Boo-backit Bridge" that you will encounter add to its pleasant old world ambience.

The ruined 14th-century Strathaven Castle peeks out from behind a curtain of trees. Only one tower and a wall survive. It changed hands many times, starting with the powerful Douglases it transferred to the Stewarts and then finally to the Hamiltons.

The castle has rather a macabre story to tell. A wife of a Lord of the castle displeased her husband so much that she was led to a purpose-built niche. She was blessed by a priest, given some food and water, and then bricked up in the niche. When a portion of the castle walls collapsed human remains were revealed, suggesting the story has some truth in it.

The castle was at the centre of activity in Covenanting times. The Covenanter Lords Montgomery, Loudon, Boyd and Lindsay seized it in 1639 when hostilities with the Royalists broke out. Later the Earl of Linlithgow garrisoned troops in the castle with the purpose of keeping down conventicles. Covenanters John Barrie and William Patterson, who are buried in the town graveyard, were shot within its walls.

Claverhouse along with his 150 dragoons stayed in Strathaven the night before their disastrous encounter with the Covenanters at

Drumclog and the banner the Covenanters carried that day in 1679 is in the towns John Hastie Museum.

The town must have grown rather fond of insurrection for, in 1820, a group of 50 "Radicals" marched from Strathaven, under the leadership of James Wilson, to Cathkin as part of a wider "Radical Rising" to protest against the introduction of the Corn Laws of 1815. The Corn Laws prevented the importation of wheat to force up its price thus sending the price of bread soaring.

Reports from Glasgow of an armed rebellion and the imminent arrival of French troops were malicious exaggerations. The Strathaven Radicals dispersed when they realised this but Wilson was arrested and tried as a traitor. He was hanged in Glasgow but his body was stolen and buried in Strathaven where he is revered as a hero. In 1846 the year the Corn Laws were repealed, a monument was erected to his memory.

A good spot for entertaining children is Strathaven's massive George Allen Park. It has been for many years a popular destination for school trips and contains all the classic day trip attractions, such as a putting green, a boating pond and a miniature steam railway. The John Hastie Museum is also within the park (open daily, afternoons only).

Practical Information

Getting There

Road: *From the south:* leave the M74 at junction 8 and follow signs for Strathaven, Stonehouse and Kilmarnock A71. *From the north:* leave the M74 at junction 6 and follow the A723 through Hamilton.

Rail: The nearest railway station that I would recommend cycling from is Hairmyres in East Kilbride, which connects to Glasgow Central. See Chapter 5 Link Routes.

Eating and Drinking

There are many options in Strathaven. There are a couple of tea-rooms on the Common Green and a number of pubs and restaurants on and around it. "The Waterside" welcomes families and provides good bar meals and real ales, just to the rear of the Common Green.

Staying

There are only B&Bs and hotels to chose from, no campsite or budget option. Contact the Tourist Information at Hamilton for assistance with booking on (01698) 285590.

14. "So many inhabited solitudes"

'So many inhabited solitudes', this is how Dorothy Wordsworth
aptly described this area when she passed through with her brother
and Coleridge. Her sentiment is especially poignant on the way to
Strathaven from Lesmahagow.

Distance: Strathaven to Lesmahagow 8 miles; Lesmahagow to Strathaven
12 miles

OS Map: Sheet 71

Terrain: The momentum from the first downhill out of Strathaven will carry
you some of the way up the hill that follows. Beyond Sandford, the route is either flat or downhill. Lesmahagow is situated deep in the Nethan Valley. The
downhill into Lesmahagow is very satisfying but the return is a climb from the
very start – but there are a couple of opportunities to get your breath back.
Once the top of the climb is attained, at over 1000 feet, the remaining cycling
is easy.

Links: This route can be linked with the other Strathaven route. Leave this
route just beyond point 8 on the Lesmahagow to Strathaven leg and join
Route 15 at point 6.

By the Way

The road roller coasts you out of Strathaven and down to the Avon but
unfortunately your momentum will not quite convey you to the top of
the rise. At the top sits the village of Sandford.

Sandford

The neat little hamlet of Sandford is entered on an iron bridge. Immediately you enter Sandford a sign points you in the direction of the peculiarly named Spectacle E'e Falls. Apparently so called because a
spurned employee placed a pair of spectacles in the thatch of the mill
adjacent to the falls. The sunlight was concentrated and a blaze
resulted, hence the name of the falls.

Sandford has some character and the overall impression is a traditional style. Indeed, a development that we pass through to leave the
village gratifyingly mimics the vernacular.

The lane that you follow out of Sandford seems at first too narrow to
go anywhere, but it is not too long before the road conspicuously
straightens and widens as it follows the course of a Roman road.

When trees and high hedges do not line the road there are good views over the hills to the south that traveller John Naismith described as "a confused group of rugged tops."

It is some distance before we turn into Boghead. A hamlet that visually reeks of its mining heritage, two neat rows of low miners' cottages line Lesmahagow Road.

The imposing Lesmahagow parish church

Lesmahagow

A fast downhill sweeps you into the small town of Lesmahagow. A rather subdued looking place today but that has not always been the case.

Lesmahagow, it seems, has always had its mind on matters ecclesiastical. In 1144, Benedictine monks from Kelso established a priory on land granted by David I. The remains of the priory can be found to the right of the Old Parish Church. The "Lesmahagow Missal" specially written for the priory in 1240 was lucky to have survived the Reformation and is now in the hands of the National Library in Edinburgh.

The Old Parish Church, built in 1804 dominates Church Square, its imposing façade was no doubt intended to intimidate the unfaithful.

Lesmahagow was a hotbed of Covenanting activity. At one point soldiers were permanently stationed in the town to control unrest. Numerous Covenanters, some of whom died in bizarre circumstances, are buried or commemorated in the churchyard.

The oldest building in Lesmahagow is the Craignethan Hotel, also on Church Square, with a lintel displaying the date 1633. Two cafés on the Main Street or a picnic in the park are the options for eating. There are also a number of pubs in the village.

To leave Lesmahagow requires a climb and it is not long before you are in the kind country that Dorothy Wordsworth was referring to. Yes there are frequent farms but the overall feeling is one of solitude.

Waterside is a particularly pleasant spot. An attractive cottage sits by the Logan Water and trees shade a substantial sandstone bridge. A signpost points uphill to yet another Covenanter Monument. It commemorates the capture and treacherous execution of David Steel by Lieutenant Crichton and the Highland Light Infantry. His descendent and namesake was the first Presiding Officer of the Scottish Parliament.

A long but not too demanding climb takes you to over 1000 feet. All the time the feeling of isolation grows, at the summit the view to the Central Belt will either disappoint or reassure you. A very fast downhill carries you for three miles through Deadwaters to the B7086.

You leave the B7086 at the first opportunity to enjoy the quiet lanes that link the substantial farms to the south of Strathaven before descending to the Avon, then climbing into the town itself.

The Route

Strathaven to Lesmahagow

Grid Ref.	Miles	Details of Route
1. 702 445	0	Start: Strathaven Common Green. Leave Common Green on Bridge Street, at top end of green passing the Boo-Backit Bridge. Emerge at T-junction opposite castle.
2. 704 445		Turn right and then left at Castle Tavern. Follow Todshill Road to T-junction.
3. 704 443		Turn left onto Lesmahagow Road and continue past Fire Station. Fast downhill leads you out of Strathaven down to bridge over Avon. Climb moderately away from Avon.
4. 718 429	1¼	At the top of the hill turn left at crossroads signed for "Sandford ¼, Stonehouse 3". Cross iron bridge and turn right in Sandford and follow road uphill past village green to T-junction.
5. 719 430		At T-junction turn right and leave Sandford on level road. Ignoring side roads follow road for 3 miles. At the end of long shelter-belt road takes sharp right and descends, followed by a short rise to T-junction with B7086.
6. 761 420	4½	Turn left onto B7086 and gently descend past entrances to quarries and into the village of Boghead.
7. 778 421	5½	In the village of Boghead turn right onto Lesmahagow Road. Lined with low cottages. Leave Boghead on the downhill. Downhill gets faster and road swings to the right signed "Lesmahagow 1½". Enter Lesmahagow on the downhill. Go under walkway linking the high school campuses to T-junction.
8. 814 403	8	Turn right and proceed into Lesmahagow.
9. 814 398	8	End: Church Square, Lesmahagow.

Lesmahagow to Strathaven

Grid Ref.	Miles	Details of Route
1ˣ. 814 398	0	Start: Lesmahagow, Church Square. Turn right onto Main Street and take first left at community library onto Bakers Brae.
2ˣ. 813 399		At the top of Bakers Brae turn left onto New Trows Road. Climb moderately out of Lesmahagow past entrance to Birkwood Hospital.
3ˣ. 807 392	¾	As gradient eases 300 metres beyond entrance to

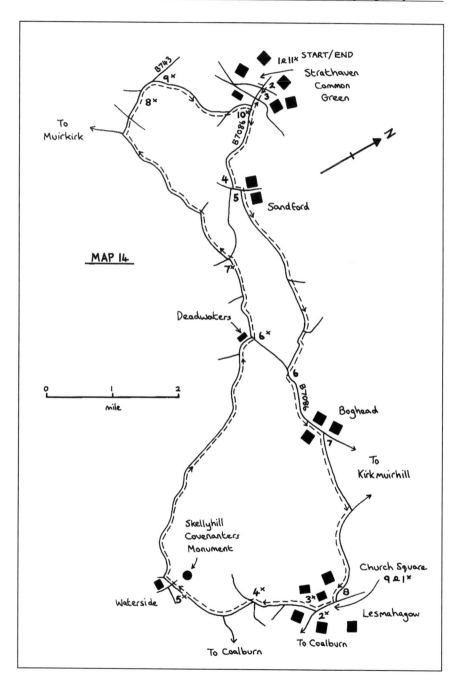

MAP 14

0   1   2
|----------|----------|
        mile

hospital turn right, signed "Waterside 2, Strathaven 10". Narrow red road and high hedges. Moderate uphill past Birkwood Mains followed by a sharp left then right.

4^x.	803 386	1¼	When straight on is indicated as a dead-end, turn left. Proceed gently downhill past Middletown Farm and Divity.
5^x.	790 371	3	Faster downhill to Waterside, continue straight on signed "Strathaven 8". (Skellyhill Covenanter Monument is to the right). Road rises to over 1000 feet topping out at the Brackenridge Farms. Long descent takes you to T-junction with B7086 at Deadwaters
6^x.	751 417	6	Turn left and follow B7086 for about 1 mile by-passing Yardbent and Castlebrocket.
7^x.	732 421	7	Take innocuous left on bend, "Give Way" sign only indication. Follow level road, going round to the right at Westhouse (old signpost points Muirkirk to the left). Cross straight over Roman road and continue to T-junction with B743.
8^x.	687 422	10	Turn right downhill and over River Avon.
9^x.	687 426	10¼	Take right immediately after crossing bridge and climb moderately. Road becomes twisty and descends into Strathaven on Newtown Road. Emerge at T-junction opposite Fire Station.
10^x.	704 442	12	Turn left at Fire Station and follow road round to the right, signed "Kilmarnock, East Kilbride, Paisley" onto Todshill Street past castle and Drumclog Arms. At T-junction go straight over and dismount pushing bike down pedestrian section to Common Green
11^x.	702 445	12	End: Strathaven Common Green.

15. Following the Avon into Ayrshire

A delightful cycle that rates as one of my favourites. Following the Avon upstream you make a brief incursion into Ayrshire skirting the striking landmark of Loudoun Hill.

Distance: 17½ miles

OS Map: Sheet 71

Terrain: Nothing more than undulations on this route, only one of which is noticeably steep.

Links: The two Strathaven rides can be linked, see Route 14.

By the Way

The quiet lane on which you leave Strathaven, except for a short dash on the A71, sets the tone for the whole day. There are no villages or towns en-route but the day is still entertaining. The gently undulating road bumps alongside the Avon Water, providing perfectly peaceful and carefree cycling. A striking feature is the number of abandoned and ruined cottages and farms that sit by the road.

Early in the route a turn on the left is signed "Kilmarnock A71"; follow it for a short distance and you arrive in the hamlet of Gilmourton. The local pub is the Bow Butts Inn; it has a large lunch menu and good beer on offer. Maybe it has come a bit early on the way round this route, but there is nothing else on offer until you return to Strathaven.

The bridge over the Glengavel Water is particularly pleasant and picturesque, and you may want to dwell a while. Not far from here, in the trees to the left (as you look upstream) is the former Dungavel Prison, once a residence of the Duke of Hamilton and the supposed destination of the Nazi Rudolf Hess when his plane crashed near Eaglesham.

Where you leave the A71, Robert the Bruce won a morale-boosting victory in 1307. Defeating Aymer de Valence, this was the second battle Bruce won after his return to Scotland from Rathlin Island.

The distinctive landmark of Loudoun Hill looms to your left, its volcanic bluffs are very popular with local rock climbers. An excellent viewpoint, it was probably used to warn of approaching enemies and probably the reason for the proximity of two battle sites.

Further on, at Mosside, limekilns can be seen in the hillside opposite a low white cottage. Just beyond Mosside, a short detour takes you to the site of the Battle of Drumclog, where a large obelisk commemorates what was arguably the Covenanters' finest hour. Just short of the battle site is a further but more practical memorial, a former seminary, built by the Duke of Hamilton for the education of ministers. It indicates the importance attached to the events of June 1679. John Graham of Claverhouse (Bonnie Dundee) was patrolling for conventicles with 150 dragoons. They stayed the night before the battle in Strathaven, so the Covenanters would have had plenty of time to prepare, deliberately selecting soft ground on which to hold their conventicle, so as to thwart the horsemen. Claverhouse and his troops attacked the armed conventicle. 30 dragoons were killed and Claverhouse himself was knocked from his horse. He skilfully mounted his dead trumpeter's horse and made his getaway. It was a skirmish rather than a battle, but a huge boost to the Covenanters' cause. Three weeks later, 4000 supporters converged on the banks of the Clyde at Hamilton only to be routed at Bothwell Brig by the Duke of Monmouth.

The return to Strathaven is by the gentlest of routes, wild-flowered verges encroach onto the already narrow lane and high hedges shelter you from unfavourable winds. The cycle alongside the Calder Water is especially pleasant, as the road is level and well sheltered. A circuitous route into Strathaven is necessary to continue on the quiet lanes and avoid the A71.

Towards Calder Water

The Route

Grid Ref.	Miles	Details of Route
1. 702 445	0	Start: Strathaven Common Green.Leave Common Green on Bridge Street, at top end of green, passing the "Boo-Backit Bridge". Emerge at T-junction opposite castle.
2. 704 445		Turn right and then left at Castle Tavern. Follow Todshill Road to T-junction.
3. 704 443		Turn left onto Lesmahagow Road.
4. 704 442	¼	Take next right at Fire Station onto Newton Road and follow out of Strathaven. Road gently rises to the right and then descends moderately to T-junction with B743.
5. 687 426	1½	Turn left and cross Avon on substantial bridge.
6. 687 423		Warning triangle warns of impending right turn. Take right turn, unsigned. Follow this road ignoring all side roads. (Continue past first sign for "A71 Kilmarnock" this is also the turning for Gilmourton and Bow Butts Inn).
7. 649 371	6	Road eventually descends to a not-obvious T-junction with B745. Signed left for "Muirkirk 7½" and right for "Kilmarnock B745". Turn right and cross narrow bridge Go straight on which effectively means turning off B745 onto minor road, signing not clear. Follow road round house on mound. Continue along delightful road. Cross hump-backed sandstone bridge. Once round bend descend to T-junction.
8. 613 371	8½	At T-junction turn left onto A71 make 100 metre dash along A71 and turn right at entrance to sand and gravel works. Battle site.
9. 617 397	10½	Road rises away from Mosside. Take next left ½ mile beyond Mosside (straight on for Battle of Drumclog).
10. 611 401	11	After ½ mile you come to a second T-junction at large white farm buildings. Turn right. Follow very pleasant road across conifer planted moorland and then alongside the Calder Water, ignoring all side roads, to crossroads.
11. 647 433	14	At crossroads go straight over signed "Strathaven 4". Road gently rises and falls.
12. 684 442	16	At next junction turn left (if you find yourself on the A71 you've gone too far). After a short rise turn right (left dead-end) descend into Strathaven past Lethame House Equestrian Centre and through residential area to crossroads opposite Common Green.
13. 702 445	17½	End: Strathaven, Common Green.

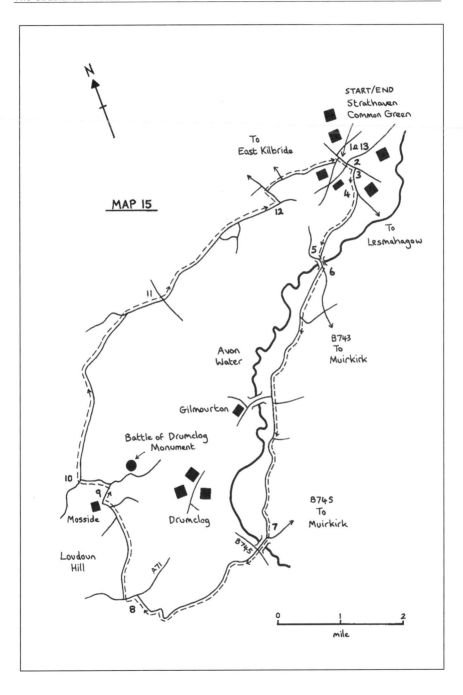

The Abington Routes

Abington Background

Abington is a surprisingly pleasant little village despite being sandwiched between the M74 and the West Coast Main Line.

To the south of Abington the Clyde Valley is narrow but the views to the north east towards Tinto are extensive. The Iron Age forts that litter the hillside that surround Abington, the traces of a Roman camp and fortlet and the motte and bailey just to the north of Abington all suggest that this was a strategically important point in the Clyde Valley. The valley floor though was avoided, indeed the Romans chose a circuitous route for their otherwise straight road on the opposite hillside, as they would have been vulnerable to ambush had they chosen the simple route.

It was the politically influential Colebrooks who created the little estate village of Abington, in the more stable 19th century, and the over-all impression is of tidy uniformity about the village centre.

Practical Information

Getting There

Road

From Lanark: follow the A73, signed Abington and Carlisle. *From Edinburgh:* take the cross country A702 via Biggar and Coulter. *From Glasgow or Carlisle:* leave the M74 at junction 13.

Eating and Drinking

Abington does not offer much in the way of amenities but the visitor is shown consideration. There is an adequate store with a tea-room, optimistically named the Abington Bistro, attached. The Abington Hotel is an impressive hangover from the days when travellers from the south had to go through rather than past. A mile to the north of the village there is a large motorway service station with all the usual facilities. It is predictably soulless but it may provide a more convenient starting point as it is handier for the northbound cycle-path.

The view north to Tinto from Abington

Staying

There are about five B&Bs or hotels in and around Abington and Crawford. There is also a campsite in Abington. The Tourist Information Centre at Abington Motorway Services will be happy to provide details and bookings, contact on (01864) 502436 or abington@seeglasgow.com. There is a SYHA Youth Hostel at Wanlockhead (Route 18) open from the end of March to November, contact on (01659) 74252.

16. Both Banks of the Clyde

A good ride for the family, wobbly cyclists young and old will feel safe, as will parents with very young children on tow. It's out to Crawford on a quiet lane on the right bank of the Clyde and then return via the cycle lane on the left bank. The day's destination of Crawford is not long coming either, just right for short attention spans.

Distance: 7 miles

OS Map: Sheet 72

Terrain: The road rises and falls but the ascents are short and undemanding.

Links: You may want to extend this ride with a trip out to the Camps Reservoir or the Midlock Valley. Both rides are also family friendly.

By the Way

The road or, rather, lane between Abington and Crawford is a very pleasant surprise. It seems to fulfil no particular purpose and its barely discernible pale yellow representation on the OS makes it a very quiet road indeed. The unfenced road winds its way over and under the railway line and provides good open views over the hillsides to the left. Crawford is usually visible, so claims that it is "just round the next bend" or "just a little further" will sound credible to young ears.

In one section the road runs very close to the railway and there is the potential for a big fright. The trains seem to be able to sneak up on the unsuspecting cyclist and they are very fast in this section.

There is a picnic area with tables just at the top of the final rise on the outward leg. At the T-junction just beyond the picnic area, at which you are directed to turn right for Crawford, you may wish to take the left and cycle the few hundred yards to view Castle Crawford (also the direction for Camps Reservoir).

Castle Crawford

Castle Crawford or as it is sometimes known Lindsay Tower after the family who occupied it, is in a dangerous and ruinous state. Built in the 17th century, it utilises the site of an earlier motte. Set amongst mature deciduous trees it almost blends in with the undergrowth. Legend has it that James V held an unusual dinner party here. The dinner guests each had a covered plate placed before them. After "grace" they removed the covers to reveal piles of silver mined from the nearby Lowther Hills.

Crawford

Crawford is an ancient settlement, the Romans built a fort nearby and Robert II elevated it to a Burgh of Barony in 1370. The symbol of Crawford's right to hold markets is its Mercat Cross, which stands on a grassy traffic island at the point at which you appear in Crawford. The central column is believed to be the real thing, but some reports suggest that it is a discarded gravestone, nonetheless it is a 'B' listed monument.

Strung out along what used to be the main road south its character is defined by more modern forms of transport. The first building that will strike you is the dilapidated Post Horn Hotel, an indication that Crawford's hey day is past. There is an attractive village centre with a post office/newsagent and a grocer who sells hot food

The town became a tourist destination with the arrival of the railway even although it sits at 900 feet above sea level and can be a very cold spot. Easily reached from both Glasgow and Edinburgh it was popular for angling and picnics on the Clyde. Crawford has always been a well used staging post. The Crawford Inn had many famous patrons, among them were Sir Robert Peel, Henry, the Duke of Bordeaux (rightful heir to the French Crown) and Prince Louis Napoleon Bonaparte.

Its location between two junctions of the M74 ensures that Crawford is popular with motorists and lorry drivers determined to avoid motorway service fare – there are a couple of cafés and a few hotels and B&Bs.

The return via the cycle lane alongside the A702 is uninspiring but it avoids the need to retrace your footsteps – and this is what you might prefer.

A good spot for a picnic, near to Crawford

The Route

	Grid Ref.	Miles	Details of Route
1.	932 233	0	Start: Car park to the rear of the Royal Bank. Leave car park as directed and turn left downhill cross bridge over Clyde and then ascend over railway line.
2.	937 232	¼	Just beyond campsite turn right at T-junction (left for golf course). Follow quiet lane running parallel to railway line. Take care when going under railway, visibility poor.
3.	953 214	3¾	Road rolls up to T-junction. Turn right for Crawford (left for Castle Crawford). Cross green bridge over Clyde. Ascend short uphill and cross narrow railway bridge to T-junction.
4.	953 211	4	Turn right past Crawford Arms Hotel. Short rise of village to roundabout. (Left for Crawford village centre).
5.	946 205	4½	Join cycle-lane that circumnavigates the roundabout. Take exit signed Abington A702 and Clyde Valley Tourist Route. Follow cycle lane until it ends at Abington.
6.	932 233	7	End: Abington, Royal Bank of Scotland.

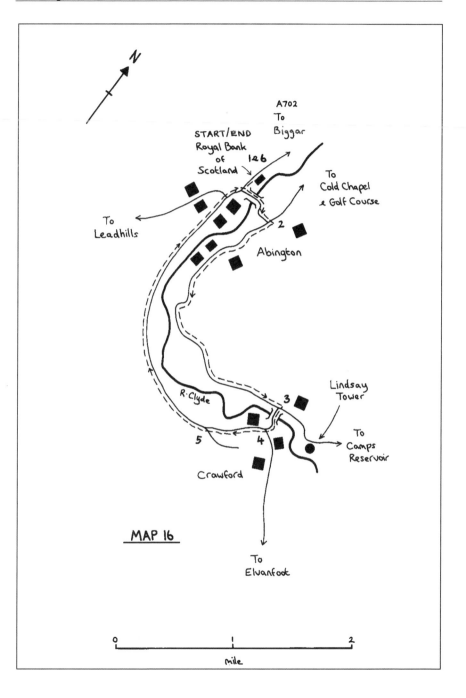

N

A702
To
Biggar

START/END
Royal Bank
of
Scotland

126

To
Cold Chapel
& Golf Course

To
Leadhills

2

Abington

R·Clyde

Lindsay
Tower

3

To
Camps
Reservoir

5

4

Crawford

MAP 16

To
Elvanfoot

0   1   2
mile

17. The Duneaton Valley and Crawfordjohn

A circular excursion to the north of Abington, you wend your way through the peaceful valley of the Duneaton Water to the historic hamlet of Crawfordjohn.

Distance: 10 miles

OS Map: Sheet 72

Terrain: It is a gradual climb from Abington to Crawfordjohn and it pauses frequently. A dip separates Crawfordjohn from the cycle-path back to Abington but once you're on the cycle-path its downhill all the way.

Links: Extend the trip to Scotland's highest villages (Route 18) by following this route as far as Crawfordjohn. At the crossroads in Crawfordjohn, just beyond the Colebrook Arms, follow the sign for Leadhills rather than Abington. It adds another climb that local cyclists refer to as the Apache Pass. At the T-junction after a long descent turn right for Leadhills or left to return to Abington.

By the Way

Once onto the cycle-path the brief brush with the M74 is easily forgotten, however it is not long until we leave the cycle-path and enter the valley of Duneaton Water. You will quickly become engrossed in the cycle through this valley. This cosy, sheltered, easy to miss valley has been the preferred home for many people down through the ages and the evidence on Black Hill (the hill on the right) suggests that it was once well populated.

Content as you may be just to cycle there is a pottery to visit, discreetly situated in the trees.

Beyond Gilkerscleugh Mains it's over the Duneaton Water for the climb into Crawfordjohn.

Crawfordjohn

Well known for a time for the manufacture of curling stones, made from essexite. When Crawfordjohn first comes into view you may think that the cold grey curling stone provides a suitable metaphor for the village as it huddles on the edge of a wide expanse of moorland.

The feeling on the inside is one of a snug, wee village with roads between houses only as wide as they absolutely need to be. The Colebrook Arms in the village will provide warmth and refreshment should it be required.

An ecclesiastical site since medieval times, Crawfordjohn was the preferred base of the convenanting regiment, the Cameronians after the settlement of 1690. The austere bleak landscape may have appealed to their puritan outlook and the need for penance. Crawfordjohn Kirk is now a heritage centre and will give the visitor an overview of the area and its people.

John McMillan became minister to the Cameronians at a time when they were trying to re-kindle the mood of revolution and religious fervour of 'The Killing Times'. At a conventicle in 1712, attended by thousands, McMillan renewed the Covenants and ex-communicated Queen Anne, an act that would have guaranteed martyrdom before 1690. On this occasion it was simply ignored.

The road between Crawfordjohn and the cycle-path tops out at above 1000 feet as Crawfordjohn is already high there is not much of a climb involved but the road does cross bleak and exposed moorland. Fortunately the cycle-path is in the main downhill into Abington.

Crawfordjohn

The Route

Grid Ref.	Miles	Details of Route
1. 932 233	0	Start: Car park to the rear of the Royal Bank. Leave car park as directed and turn right, then right again. Follow main thoroughfare out of village to roundabout.
2. 931 247	¾	At roundabout join cycle-path. Follow cycle-lane "Route 74-North". Follow road signs for "Douglas B7078" uphill over M74.
3. 928 246	1	At second roundabout follow cycle-lane and then cross B7078 to join cycle-path (traffic free). Cycle path rises and then descends gently to turning for "Crawfordjohn 3¾".
4. 918 249	1¾	Take left turn for Crawfordjohn and descend towards Duneaton Bridge. Follow undulating road running parallel to Duneaton Water. Road passes through conifer woodland and then eventually descends to cross the Duneaton Water.
5. 897 240	4¼	At T-junction just beyond bridge turn left onto Manse Road and ascend into Crawfordjohn. Go through Crawfordjohn to 4-way junction with B740 just beyond Colebrook Arms.
6. 879 238	5¼	Turn right onto B740 signed "Abington 5". Follow rising dyke lined road away from Crawfordjohn. Road tops out at about 1000 feet. Road then dips and then rises to T-junction with B7078 and cycle-path.
7. 891 259	7	Turn right onto cycle-path and follow "Route 74- South". Cycle-path descends more or less all the way to roundabout. Cross B7078 and follow cycle-lane, avoiding roundabout, to second roundabout. Continue to follow cycle lane to its conclusion and return into Abington.
8. 932 233	10	End: Abington, Royal Bank of Scotland.

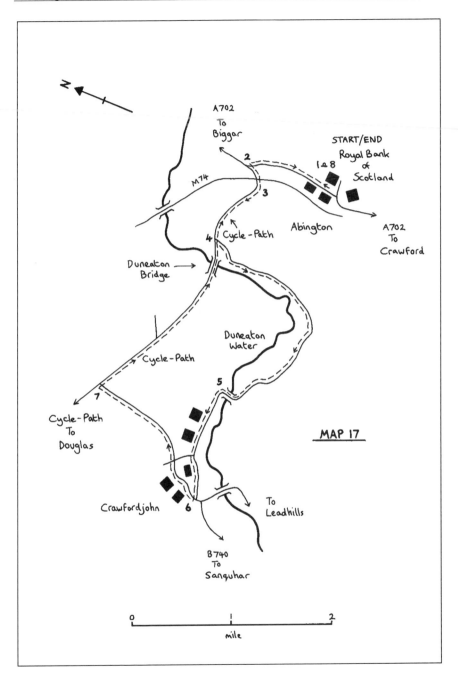

N

A702
To
Biggar

START/END
Royal Bank
of
Scotland

1 & 8

2

M74

3

4 Cycle-Path

Abington

A702
To
Crawford

Duneaton
Bridge

Duneaton
Water

Cycle-Path

5

7

Cycle-Path
To
Douglas

MAP 17

To
Leadhills

Crawfordjohn

6

B740
To
Sanquhar

0   1   2

mile

18. God's Treasure House in Scotland

From Abington you climb deep into the Lowther Hills to Scotland's highest villages Wanlockhead and Leadhills. Two villages that are to all intents open air museums. Both villages are littered with vivid reminders of their lead mining past

Distance: 19 miles

OS Maps: 72 and 78

Terrain: This is a very entertaining route so don't be put off by the fact that you are cycling to Scotland's highest villages. The climbs are sustained but not particularly steep. Get off and push if you feel you have to.

Links: Can be linked to Route 5 for a long cycle from Lanark to Wanlockhead (follow A72 from Roberton to Abington) and returning via Douglas. Extend this route by following Route 17 as far as Crawfordjohn and take the hill road to the south signed Leadhills.

By the Way

Almost immediately after leaving Abington you become enveloped in hills, rounded heathery hillsides gradually close in on you as you ascend towards Leadhills. For a road that climbs to over 1500 feet it does not climb as ferociously as might have been feared. The climb is noticeable once we are joined from the left by the road from Crawfordjohn, a hill road that local cyclists refer to as the Apache Pass.

The first signs of mining activity appear, old bridges, wagon ways and spoil heaps dot the heathery slopes. In the distance is the Civil Aviation Authority's radar station in the recognisable form of a giant golf ball on the summit of Green Lowther you will find yourself not far short of it when you reach Wanlockhead.

Leadhills

Leadhills is every bit the mining village. It has an endearing informality and the village feels little changed. Terraced villas and cottages in pastel colours line un-surfaced roads. This is a factory village with no grand plan.

The well-known mathematician Stirling, a popular and forward-thinking mine manager in the 18th century, along with the Pentland Poet Allan Ramsay, a native of Leadhills, instituted what is

Leadhills: the "Curfew Bell" of 1770, which sounded the change of shift and emergencies

regarded to be Scotland's oldest subscription library in 1741. The library, on Main Street is still in use today as a reference library and has other interesting exhibits on display.

Abandon Main Street for Ramsay Road to get a proper feel for the village. A road curves off Ramsay Road to the graveyard. A headstone states that John Taylor lived to the remarkable age of 137 years. No date of birth or death is given. Hmm!

Just over the wall from John Taylor's grave is an obelisk erected to the memory and achievements of local lad William Symington, the first person to build and design a boat propelled by a steam engine. He was ahead of his time and died penniless.

Near the centre of the village, on a slight promontory, is the curfew bell, suspended from pyramidal supports it carries the date 1770. The bell would peel between shifts but now it only heralds the New Year and the occasional emergency.

Wanlockhead is one mile further on and 200 feet further up. But if you don't fancy the cycle, you can take the narrow gauge steam railway, a remnant of the line that ran from the main line at Elvanfoot to Wanlockhead until 1939.

Cycling between Leadhills and Wanlockhead there are more reminders of the area's mining past. Tumbledown buildings and more spoil heaps litter the hillsides but they do seem to add to the landscape rather than detract from it. Zinc and lead extraction may have sustained these communities until 1957 but it was gold that attracted the atten-

Wanlockhead

tion of the Scottish Kings James IV, V, VI – even Queen Elizabeth I had the area mined on her behalf. Large quantities of gold being mined led to the area being nicknamed "God's Treasure House in Scotland". This was probably a ploy by royalty to give it an owner not of this world so that they could act as its earthly custodians. The Honours of Scotland on display in Edinburgh Castle are made from gold mined in this area. The World Gold Panning Championships are frequently held in the Lowther Hills.

Wanlockhead

Wanlockhead lies just over the watershed in Galloway. Bizarrely the crests of the hills that mark the boundary, were viewed as no-mans land and so the locale became the burial site for many suicide victims, who were brought from all over.

Wanlockhead sits in a hollow, the houses rise up the sides but don't mange to spill out. On a fine day Wanlockhead looks idyllic but it is very cold in winter. I have cycled along roads cleared of deep snow as early as October.

Wanlockhead is a fascinating village. The formal side of the visitor experience is the Lead Mining Museum, which provides an opportunity to go underground, pan for gold, and visit the Miner's Library and typical Miner's cottage. It is enough just to wander the track beds. Wagons sit on rails frozen in time at the entrance to boarded up pits. An old beam engine used for pumping water from the mines still sits in its place. Huge grey 'bings' (spoil heaps) tower over smelting works and abandoned mine buildings. All of which combine to give Wanlockhead a very authentic atmosphere.

To have to climb out of the hollow to rejoin the road back to Leadhills does not seem fair after reaching such a high point. The downhill into Leadhills is short lived as you have to climb again through a narrow rocky pass at 1300 feet. Beyond the pass five sensational miles of cycling, that keep you above 1000 feet, of rolling red road, accompanied by the babbling Elvan Water. The track bed of the dismantled narrow gauge railway criss-crosses your route. Tourists would flock to enjoy such a rail journey today but it is unlikely ever to be possible as a plaque by the side of the road laments the demolition of the impressive Risping Viaduct.

At Elvanfoot you emerge out of the hills into the Clyde Valley. This is the point at which the Romans first encountered and crossed the Clyde. The cycle path that follows the M74 is functional and relatively safe and it is undoubtedly the most efficient means of returning to Abington. If you prefer the back lanes and proximity to the hills, leave the cycle path for Crawford and turn right at the dilapidated Post Horn Hotel, cross the Clyde and turn left for Abington (the reverse of the first leg of Both Sides of the Clyde, Route 16).

The Route

Grid Ref.	Miles	Details of Route
1. 932 233	0	Start: Car park to the rear of the Royal Bank. Leave car park as directed and turn right and then left at T-junction.
2. 930 231	¼	Proceed up short rise and take next right, signed "Leadhills, Wanlockhead, Sanquhar B797" and cross over motorway.
3. 902 207	2¼	Cycling is easy until Caravan Club site at Lettershaw then road climbs for at least 3 miles into Leadhills. Climb through Leadhills on Main Street or on Ramsay Road.
4. 878 132	7	Continue along road for a further mile to the village of Wanlockhead.
5. 887 153	8½	Return to Leadhills. Turn right at Leadhills Primary School, signed "Elvanfoot B7040". Climb through rocky pass and then follow rising and dipping road to T-junction with A702.
6. 951 174	13	Turn left at T-junction on A702. (Elvanfoot and pedestrian bridge over the Clyde straight ahead via Village Road).
7. 956 186	14	At roundabout take first exit signed "Crawford B7076". Go under motorway and join separate cycle-path.
8. 960 200	15	At Crawford either turn right to go through Crawford to rejoin cycle-path at far side or just continue to follow the cycle-path to Abington.
9. 932 233	19	End: Royal Bank of Scotland, Abington.

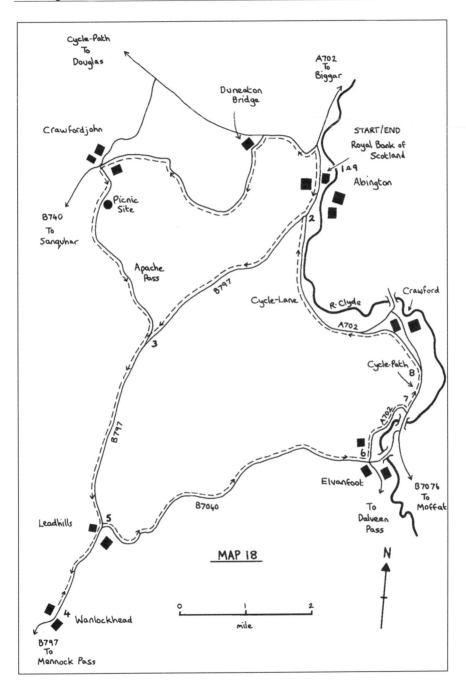

MAP 18

The Reservoir Routes

These routes may appeal to families who want to cycle together or to those who want to build up their confidence. They all follow dead-end roads, so traffic is light. You should still take care as others may assume that they are also unlikely to encounter other road users.

In each case you travel deep into what would otherwise be obscure valleys, were it not for the reservoirs. This may have led people from earlier times to choose these valleys as their home. The hillsides around Nisbet and Snaip on the way to the Coulter Reservoirs have abundant remnants of Iron Age forts and settlements and the Camps Reservoir revealed a Bronze Age cemetery during a recent dry spell. The OS map shows evidence of at least a dozen ancient settlements in the Midlock Valley. Flints found around the Daer Reservoir date to the Mesolithic Period – the earliest evidence of human occupation of Lanarkshire.

As these reservoirs provide a large part of Lanarkshire with their water supply, certain rules should be observed:

❣ No bathing

❣ No picnics near the reservoirs

❣ No fishing without a permit

❣ Do not approach the reservoirs, especially around the Daer Reservoir as the ground is dangerously soft.

19. Coulter and Cowgill Reservoirs

Distance: Coulter Village to Coulter Reservoir, 4½ miles; Coulter Village to Cowgill Reservoir, 4 miles

OS Map: Sheet 72

Terrain: It is uphill to the reservoirs but it is a very gradual ascent. Not far out of Coulter the way is blocked by a short steep pull, see below to avoid it.

Short cuts: To avoid the climbs early in the route start from Birthwood where car parking is provided primarily for those wishing to climb Culter Fell.

Getting There: Coulter Village straddles the A702 just 2 miles south of Biggar. If arriving from the north follow the directions for Biggar. From the south leave the M74 at junction 13, Abington. Follow signs for Biggar A702, turning left 1 mile from motorway services. Seven or eight miles later you come to Coulter.

Links: You can extend this route by starting from Biggar. From the Corn Exchange turn left and follow High Street to Cadgers Brig. Turn left at Cadgers Brig onto Station Road and follow it past the rugby club and Boghall Castle. At the entrance to the Hartree House Hotel turn right and after a short distance turn left. Follow the road round to the right at Thripland Farm. After one mile you arrive at a T-junction. Turn right and descend into Coulter Village.

By the Way

The trip out to the Coulter and Cowgill Reservoirs involves crossing the Southern Boundary Fault, separating the central lowlands from the Southern Uplands. On this ride the contrast could not be more stark. The two narrow, steep-sided river valleys that contain the reservoirs penetrate deep into the hills that surround Culter Fell (2445 feet) indeed much of the land is over 2000 feet.

The Cowgill Glen is small but perfectly formed and the reservoirs have a completely natural air, surrounded as they are by fir trees. Many spots in the glen scream 'picnic'! Coulter Reservoir on the other hand is at the head of a much wider valley. The dam and the new waterworks cannot be missed. It is still for the most part a journey into beautifully wild hill country an impression that is heightened should you go to the top of the dam. The road sits on the bed of a narrow gauge railway, which was built to transport puddle clay up the valley for the construction of the dam.

The Routes

Grid Ref.	Miles	Details of Route
1. 026 338	0	Start: Coulter Village Hall. Leave car park and turn left past village hall.
2. 025 338		Turn left at T-junction and leave Coulter on level road.
3. 028 332	½	Follow road to the right over bridge and take right-hand fork signed Birthwood. Road rises moderately and tops out in trees. Road falls and rises and then finally descends to Birthwood and Culter Allers.
4. 031 312	2	Just beyond Culter Allers Farm road forks. Right-hand fork for Cowgill reservoirs, left-hand fork for Coulter Reservoir.

Coulter Reservoir

037 276	4½	Following the road round to the left, past entrance to big house, and then to the right. Road climbs gently to dam, steep climb to attain the top of the dam.

The beautiful valley of the Cowgill Reservoir

Cowgill Reservoir

009 290	4	Follow level road through trees alongside burn. Road crosses two bridges followed by a short stiff climb. Now the road can be seen climbing steadily across the hillside. Road dips towards white cottage and then climbs towards dam. Road is un-surfaced but level through trees Lower Cowgill reservoir below on the right, track ends at gate just below dam. To attain the top of the dam it is necessary to continue on foot.

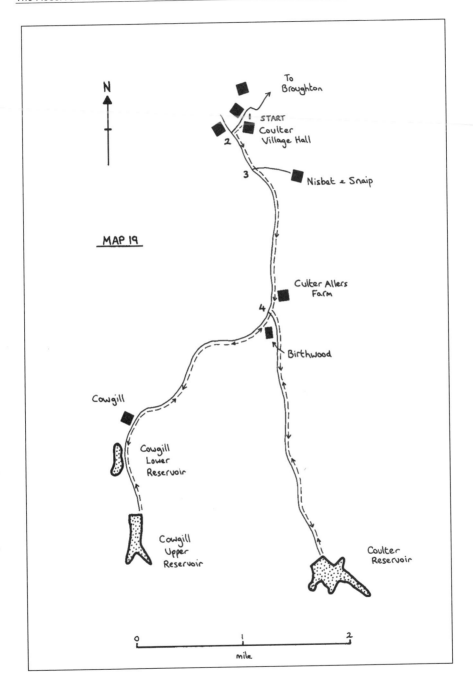

N

MAP 19

To Broughton

START
Coulter
Village Hall

1

2

3

Nisbet & Snaip

Culter Allers
Farm

4

Birthwood

Cowgill

Cowgill
Lower
Reservoir

Cowgill
Upper
Reservoir

Coulter
Reservoir

0   1   2
mile

20. Camps Reservoir and the Midlock Valley

Distance: Crawford to Camps Reservoir, 3 miles; Crawford to Midlock Valley road end, 3 miles

OS Map: Sheet 72

Terrain: Both options offer very gentle cycling.

Getting There: Crawford sits between M74 junctions 13 and 14. Leave at either for Crawford.

Links: You may want to extend this route by starting from Abington and following the direction given in Route 16 to Crawford.

By the Way

In the section common to both possibilities we pass by Castle Crawford a brief history of which is offered in Route 16, page 101. Also just before the split, the road that leaves to the left is part of the Roman road that linked the Clydesdale forts with the south.

The road to the Camps Reservoir has no discernible gradient. The surface is excellent and the wind tends to blow up this wide and open valley towards the reservoir. There is a small community at the foot of the dam. A road ascends to the crest of the dam and a rough road circumnavigates the reservoir. The construction of the dam began in 1916 and was completed in 1930. 200 German Prisoners of War were involved in the early construction work

The Midlock Valley road is just as undemanding. The road surface is not great in places but the road offers more variety as it twists and turns hugging the sides of this narrow valley. The view to the head of the valley is terrific and is nearly always visible.

The Route

	Grid Ref.	Miles	Details of Route
1.	952 209	0	Start: Crawford Arms Hotel. With your back to the hotel turn right. Turn next left and cross railway line on narrow bridge, signed Castle Crawford/Lindsay Tower. Leave Crawford on the downhill and cross Clyde via green bridge. Follow road past Castle Crawford to small collection of houses known as Midlock.
2.	962 215	¾	250 yards further on from Midlock the road forks. Right for the Midlock Valley and left for the Camps Reservoir.

Camps Reservoir

	995 225	3	Good surfaced road climbs for a short distance beyond that there is no discernible gradient. Follow road up wide valley to dam.

Midlock Valley

	987 204	3	Take the right-hand fork. Road is surfaced but rough in places. Level road takes you up narrow glen to just short of Welphill. Rough track forms a loop up to Welphill and through the farmyard and returns via downhill on grassy track beyond sheep pens.

An easy return from the Camps Reservoir

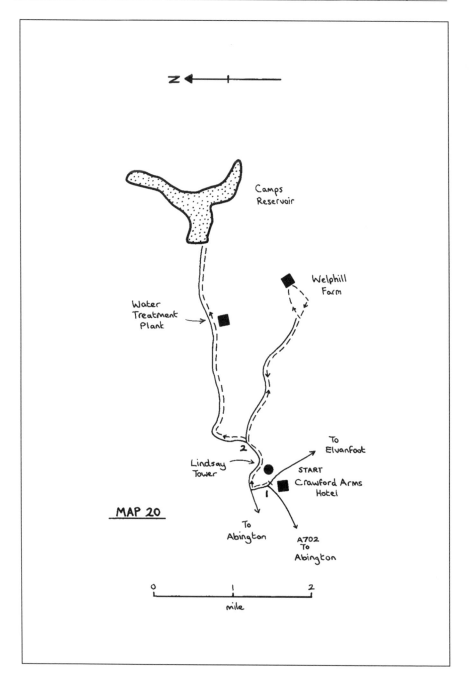

Camps Reservoir

Welphill Farm

Water Treatment Plant

To Elvanfoot

Lindsay Tower

START Crawford Arms Hotel

MAP 20

To Abington

A702 To Abington

0   1   2
mile

21. Daer Reservoir and the source of the Clyde

Distance: A702 to foot of dam, 3 miles; A702 to Kirkhope Farm, 6 miles

OS Map: Sheet 78

Terrain: Easy enough to the foot of the dam. A steep climb is necessary to get to the top of the dam but it is fairly easy beyond the dam with only a couple of short rises to deal with.

Getting There: Leave the M74 at junction 14 and follow A702 signed Drumlanrig Castle and Thornhill. Follow A702 for about 3 miles beyond Elvanfoot. Car park for Glenochar Heritage Trail is on the right ½ mile before turning for Daer Reservoir.

By the Way

This is, as they say, a ride of two halves. The first half is an undemanding cycle to the foot of the dam where there are two great picnic spots, one by the commemorative cairn and the other by the stone bridge. Both are just beyond the junction at the foot of the dam.

To progress beyond the dam a steep pull has to be endured but once you are at the top you will feel it is was worthwhile. There is a real feeling of remoteness and emptiness. The road reaches its terminus at Kirkhope Farm, which would appear to be in an unsustainably remote location. Queensbury Hill, the highest point behind the farm, is the source of the Clyde. The hills that surround the farm provide a backdrop that gives the sense of a high alpine valley.

The Route

	Grid Ref.	Miles)	Details of Route
1.	951 133	0	Start: Junction of A702 and road signed Daer Waterworks. Follow rising and falling road to entrance of West of Scotland Water premises. Commemorative cairn just beyond junction.
2.	972 097	3	At junction turn right and descend to bridge before ascending steeply for a short distance to gain top of dam. Follow more or less level road along reservoir side to road end at Kirkhope.
3.	963 054	6	Road End at Kirkhope.

The lonely Kirkhope Farm and Queensbury Hill beyond, the source of the Clyde

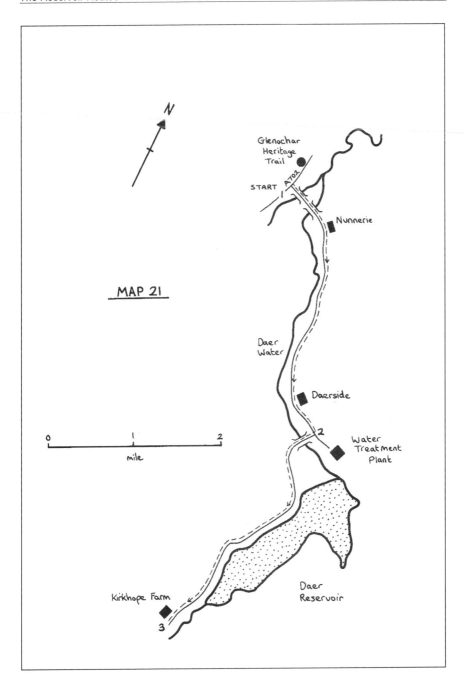

N

Glenochar
Heritage
Trail

START A702

MAP 21

Nunnerie

Daer
Water

Daerside

2

Water
Treatment
Plant

0   1   2
        mile

Daer
Reservoir

Kirkhope Farm

3

Link Routes and Further Afield

1. Hairmyres Railway Station, East Kilbride to Strathaven (11 miles)

This is a signed cycle route from East Kilbride to Strathaven and a leaflet describing the route in detail with an accompanying map is available from South Lanarkshire Council. Some of the signs do not point the way they are supposed to, due to practical jokers – so don't rely on them.

Leave Hairmyres Station, turn right and leave car park at roundabout, take second exit. There then follow three roundabouts go straight through the next two, at the third take the left, signed Gardenhall and Mossnuek, onto Greenhills Road. Follow Greenhills Road for about one mile. At next roundabout turn right onto Newlands Road and go straight through at next roundabout. Pass through area where streets are named after Lake District landmarks. Suddenly Newlands Road narrows to single track and enters open countryside at Newlands Farm. After a short distance you arrive at a T-junction turn left, signed as a cycleway. You skirt new housing and eventually come to another T-junction turn left signed East Kilbride. Continue to skirt new housing for about ¾ mile and turn right onto short rough road through a small copse of trees to T-junction; turn right and follow the road into Auldhouse. Turn right (opposite Auldhouse Arms) and then immediately left onto Cleuchearn Road. At next T-junction turn left, signed Strathaven 6 miles. Continue past turning for Darvel and through Leaburn. At Millwell Farm turn left. Follow the road for one mile to T-junction and turn right at Dykehead Farm. Follow the road round to the right at North Carnduff Farm and take right fork shortly afterwards. Road continues downhill, turn right at the junction where two shelter belts meet at right angles. After 400 yards turn left, passing large farm with ducks. Pass Lethame House Equestrian Centre and enter Strathaven. At T-junction with Threestanes Road turn right and follow to traffic lights at Common Green.

2. Dykehead Railway Station, Shotts to Forth (6 miles)

Leave Railway Station either by ramp or via car park and turn right. At roundabout turn right signed "Newmains, Fauldhouse, Kilmarnock and Edinburgh A71". After a short distance take next left and follow road past shops and out of Shotts. Just as you leave Shotts turn left signed "Fauldhouse B7010" and re-enter Shotts on the Springhill Road. Follow road out of Shotts and continue along it for a further mile to crossroads. Cross the A71 signed "Forth 4". Follow B715 uphill past landfill and through commercial forestry, the long uphill peaks at Climpy (1000 feet). Road descends for a short distance out of Climpy and then ascends for a short distance into Forth. At the junction with Forth Main Street, go straight over onto Manse Road to start Route 7.

3. The Tweed Cycleway, Lanark or Carstairs Junction to Berwick-upon-Tweed.

The Route as far as Peebles.

The Tweed Cycleway originally ran for 90 miles from Biggar to Berwick-upon-Tweed. You may find it strange that The Tweed Cycle Way now starts in the Clyde Valley. This is because Scottish Borders is the largest region in Europe without a railway station. The stations at Lanark or Carstairs Junction are the closest to the original start point of Biggar. You can either follow Route 1 as far as Thankerton, turning right over Boat Bridge and following Tweed Cycleway signs into Biggar. Alternatively you can follow Route 13 from Carstairs Junction to Biggar.

From Biggar follow Route 9 to Broughton. In Broughton take the first left after Village Hall onto Dreva Road which climbs to an Iron Age Fort on the right, a very good viewpoint, and then onto to the cottages at Dreva. The road descends to a T-junction with the B712, turn left and follow a fairly level road through the pretty hamlet of Stobo with its ancient church and health spa.

Continue through Stobo. About 1½ miles beyond Stobo take right signed "Lyne Station 1". Just before the hump-backed bridge turn right onto a dead-end road. The road becomes track. Cross the Tweed on the footbridge and then follow the track to the left. At houses turn right onto tarmac road. Follow this road up and over a hill. At T-junction turn left signed "Peebles 4". After 400 metres turn first right signed "Peebles via Cademuir". Follow road for about 5 miles into Peebles. Follow Bonnington Road to T-junction. Turn right and then left onto Springhill Road. Turn right at the end of Springhill Road for Peebles. Turn left to continue following the Tweed Cycleway.

Useful Contacts

Tourist Information Centres

Abington: Welcome Break, Motorway Service Area (Junction 13, M74), Abington ML12 6RG, (01864) 502436; abington@seeglasgow.com

Biggar: 155 High Street , Biggar ML12 6DL, (01899) 221066

Glasgow: 11 George Square, Glasgow G2 1DY, (0141) 204 4400; enquiries@seeglasgow.com

Hamilton: Road Chef Services (M74 Northbound), Hamilton ML3 6JW, (01698) 285590; hamilton@seeglasgow.com

Lanark: Horsemarket, Ladyacre Road, Lanark ML11 7LQ, (01555) 661661; lanark@seeglasgow.com

Cycling Organisations

The Edinburgh Bike Bus, 4 Barclay Terrace, Edinburgh EH10 1DU, (0131) 228 1368. A transport service for cyclists and their bikes, it caters for local people looking for a day out or groups wanting to travel anywhere in Scotland. Bike Bus is not a holiday company nor does it provide a scheduled service.

Cyclists Touring Club, 69 Meadrow, Godalming, Surrey GU7 3HS, (01483) 417217

Spokes, The Lothian Cycle Campaign, 232 Dalry Road, Edinburgh EH11 2JG

GO Bike (Strathclyde Cycle Campaign), PO Box 15175, Glasgow G4 9LP

SUSTRANS (Scotland), 3 Coates Place, Edinburgh EH3 7AA, (0131) 623 7600. The charity that promotes and funds safe cycle routes for all, they are responsible for most of the cycle-paths and cycle routes you encounter around the country.

The South of Scotland Tandem Club, c/o Graeme and Tracey Short, Overlaw, Causeway End, Biggar; overlaw@talk21.com

Bibliography

Upper Clydesdale: A History and a Guide *by Daniel Martin*

Britannica.com

Ancient Monuments of Clydesdale, *Clydesdale District Council*

Historic Buildings of Clydesdale, *Clydesdale District Council*

Clydesdale Built, *Clydesdale District Council*

Old Tinto Villages *by Ann Matheson*

Lanarkshire: Prehistoric and Roman Monuments, *The Royal Commission on the Ancient and Historical Monuments of Scotland*

A History of Strathaven and Avondale *by William Fleming Downie*

Biggar Town Trail *by David Littlejohn*

Arthur and Merlin, The Tweedale Connection *by John Randall*

Also of Interest:

BEST PUB WALKS AROUND GLASGOW

David Hunter

26, circular, assorted walks with a selection of sights and delights to tempt even the most confirmed 'cityphile' beyond the urban limits! All accompanied by the author's own photographs and detailed sketch maps, these excellent routes cover areas such as the Antonine wall, the Forth and Clyde Canal, or the West Highland Way, with the promise of good food and drink at one of the hospitable pubs along the way. A great way to experience Scottish life past and present. £6.95

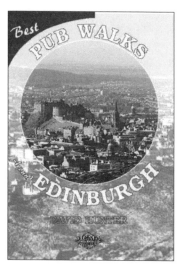

BEST PUB WALKS AROUND EDINBURGH

David Hunter

Explores the rich treasure chest of scenery and sights in Edinburgh and the splendid surrounding open country. Each of the 26 walks, ranging from 3 to 10 miles, starts and finishes at a good pub with a difference. Most of the walking is on bridleways, quiet lanes and canal towpaths, varied by the surprise of spectacular clifftop walks, leisurely river valley strolls and rewarding routes over farmland. £7.95

All of our books are available through booksellers. In case of difficulty, or for a free catalogue, please contact: SIGMA LEISURE, 1 SOUTH OAK LANE, WILMSLOW, CHESHIRE SK9 6AR.
Phone: 01625-531035   Fax: 01625-536800.
E-mail: info@sigmapress.co.uk
Web site: http//www.sigmapress.co.uk
MASTERCARD and VISA orders welcome.